LIVE FEAR FREE

KENNETH COPELAND

LIVE FEAR FREE

KENNETH COPELAND

KENNETH COPELAND
PUBLICATIONS

Unless otherwise noted, all scripture is from the *King James Version* of the Bible.

Scripture quotations marked *Amplified Bible, Classic Edition* are from the *Amplified® Bible,* © 1954, 1958, 1962, 1964, 1965, 1987 by The Lockman Foundation. Used by permission.

Scripture quotations marked *New King James Version* are from the *New King James Version* © 1982 by Thomas Nelson Inc.

Scripture quotations marked *Wuest Translation* are from *The New Testament: An Expanded Translation* by Kenneth S. Wuest © Wm. B. Eerdmans Publishing Co. 1961. All rights reserved.

Live Fear Free

ISBN 978-1-60463-602-4   30-0092

30 29 28 27 26 25   6 5 4 3 2 1

© 2025 Kenneth Copeland

Kenneth Copeland Publications
Fort Worth, TX 76192-0001

For more information about Kenneth Copeland Ministries, visit kcm.org or call 1-800-600-7395 (U.S. only) or +1-817-852-6000.

Printed in Canada. All rights reserved under International Copyright Law. No part of this book may be reproduced or transmitted in any form or by any means, electronic or mechanical, including photocopying, recording, or by any information storage and retrieval system, without the written permission of the publisher.

TABLE OF CONTENTS

CHAPTER 1
The Victory That Overcomes the World 1

CHAPTER 2
The Law of the Spirit of Life in Christ Jesus 21

CHAPTER 3
Focus on The WORD, Not the Waves 39

CHAPTER 4
Your Will, Your Choice, Your Words 59

CHAPTER 5
Applying and Acting On Your Faith....................77

CHAPTER 6
When You Stand Praying.....................................99

CHAPTER 7
The Fear-Free, Failure-Proof Life of Love........ 119

CHAPTER 8
Under the Protective Umbrella of God 139

CHAPTER 9
Safe in the Almighty Arms of Love.................... 161

CHAPTER 10
As Ashes Under Your Feet.................................. 181

CHAPTER 1

THE VICTORY THAT OVERCOMES THE WORLD

CHAPTER 1

THE VICTORY
THAT OVERCOMES
THE WORLD

This know also, that in the last days perilous times shall come.
(2 Timothy 3:1)

And it shall come to pass in the last days, saith God,
I will pour out of my Spirit upon all flesh.
(Acts 2:17)

WE ARE LIVING RIGHT NOW in what the Bible calls "the last days." We're not waiting for them to come. They're here and, as the old saying goes, they are "the best of times and the worst of times." They're days of great glory on one hand and days of great peril on the other.

They're perilous because, as this age comes to an end, the devil is fighting furiously for his survival. Seeing he only has a small sliver of time left before Jesus returns, he's using his corruptive influence in this world to cause evil men to "wax worse and worse, deceiving, and being deceived" (2 Timothy 3:13). He's a thief, and he's doing his utmost to steal, kill and destroy everything he can (John 10:10).

At the same time, however, the kingdom of God is advancing. God is pouring out His Spirit on all flesh. He's giving His people

LIVE FEAR FREE

greater revelations from His WORD. In the face of the worst the devil can do, The LORD Jesus Christ is building His Church and proving that the gates of hell cannot prevail against it.

God is teaching us, as believers, how to not only survive these last days but to thrive in them. He's turning us into living testimonies of the Love and power of God, and preparing us to help bring in the greatest harvest of souls this earth has ever seen.

Yes, these are perilous times, but for those of us who know and love Jesus, this is our finest hour!

At a time when multitudes of people are scared stiff because of all the bad news they're hearing, we get to tell them the *good news* about Jesus. At a time when people are feeling overwhelmed by all the madness in the world, we get to tell them that "whatsoever is born of God overcometh the world" (1 John 5:4). We get to be the generation that helps bring to pass what Jesus prophesied in Matthew 24:14:

> This gospel of the kingdom shall be preached in all the world for a witness unto all nations; and then shall the end come.

You can forget all the silly stuff people say about the end coming because of climate change, pandemics, famines or some man-made disaster. You can even forget what some misinformed Christian people say about how all the turmoil that's breaking out around us—the wars and rumors of war, the terrorism, political upheavals, supply shortages and economic woes—are going to stop the spread of the gospel.

It doesn't matter what *people* say. It's what *Jesus* said that matters. And He didn't say the gospel will be preached unless the terrorists take over, or the wrong political party gets in power, or

The Victory That Overcomes the World

we run out of gasoline or prices stay down like they should. No, Jesus said the gospel will be preached to all nations till the end comes. He said it will be preached *as a witness!*

Do you know what the witness to the gospel *is* in these last days?

First, let me tell you what it's not.

It's not a bunch of scared Christians buying up all the blankets, canned goods and kerosene lanterns in town; and then hiding out in a cave somewhere just hoping to survive. That isn't it. The gospel has never functioned that way, and it never will.

"The gospel…is the power of God unto salvation" (Romans 1:16)!

The gospel functions at its best right in the midst of adversity. It shines the brightest right in the face of all the impossibilities and the worst havoc satan can bring to pass on this earth.

In these last days, the witness of the gospel to the world will be believers who walk in God's power. Terrorism can't terrify them, pandemics can't rattle them, and supply shortages can't shake them. They will be Christians who go wherever God sends them, even when it looks like there's no way to get there. They'll be people of faith who have food on the table to share when there's no way in the natural to get it. They'll be generous givers who keep prospering and giving in the face of scarcity and fearlessly declare, "My God meets my needs according to His riches in glory, by Christ Jesus" (Philippians 4:19).

That kind of witness for the gospel gets people's attention. It causes unbelievers to look at you and say, "I don't know how you do it," and gives you the opportunity to tell them, "I didn't do it, Jesus did, and He'll do it for you just like He does for me!"

LIVE FEAR FREE

As a believer living on the earth in this end-time hour, you were born to be that kind of gospel witness. You don't have to be intimidated by the contrary conditions the devil is stirring up around you. You may not yet fully know how to live fearlessly and victoriously in the midst of them. But you know in your spirit that "greater is He that is in you, than he that is in the world" (1 John 4:4).

Even now, as the perils of the world swirl around you, something down on the inside of you is saying, *In Jesus, there's victory in all this! There's winning in this! There's salvation in this!*

EXCEEDING GREAT AND PRECIOUS PROMISES

"But Brother Copeland," somebody might say, "how can there be salvation for me in dealing with the dangers that are coming on the world these days? Doesn't salvation just guarantee I'll go to heaven when I die?"

No, the word *salvation* in Romans 1:16 is the Greek word *soteria* which means "to save or deliver from evil or danger of any kind: physical, including health, as well as spiritual, temporal and eternal." So, your salvation provides you with much more than a future in heaven. It provides present-day deliverance in every area of life.

In other words, the salvation that's ours, as believers in Jesus, is all-inclusive! It provides everything we need to live in victory, not just in the sweet by-and-by, but in the rugged here and now. As 2 Peter 1:3-4 says:

[God] according as his divine power hath given unto us all things that pertain unto life and godliness, through the knowledge of him that hath called us to glory and virtue:

The Victory That Overcomes the World

whereby are given unto us exceeding great and precious promises: that by these ye might be partakers of the divine nature, having escaped the corruption that is in the world through lust.

Notice those verses aren't written in future tense. They don't say that someday we'll escape this world and go to be with Jesus. They say we've been given God's promises so we can *be* (present tense) partakers of the divine nature, having *escaped* (past tense) the corruption that is in the world through lust.

The corruption that's in this world through lust isn't just the moral corruption that's so rampant these days. It's all the evil that's here because of mankind's sin. It includes all the destruction that was released into the earth when Adam surrendered his God-given authority to the devil in the Garden of Eden.

People who have no Covenant with God have no defense against that destruction. They have no way to escape the fear it casts over their lives. But, as believers, we do! Through the salvation that's ours in Jesus, and God's exceeding great and precious promises, we can live fearlessly and victoriously in this world. We can go right on, even in perilous times, enjoying life and life more abundantly!

But if that's the case, you might wonder, *why don't we see more Christians doing it? Why do we see so many sincere believers being overtaken by the same destruction that's overtaking the unbelievers in the world?*

It's certainly not because it's God's will.

If it had been His will, He wouldn't have sent Jesus. He wouldn't have filled His written WORD with His promises of protection, healing, prosperity and BLESSING in every area of

LIVE FEAR FREE

life. But He did. So, obviously, if we, as Christians, aren't experiencing those BLESSINGS, God is not the problem.

What *is* the problem? God told us in Hosea 4:6: "My people are destroyed for lack of knowledge."

What knowledge is lacking? The knowledge of God's exceeding great and precious promises. The knowledge of how to operate by faith in those promises and to refusing to fear.

"Well, I'm all for faith," someone might say, "but you have to be realistic. In this crazy world, we just can't help being afraid sometimes."

We can if we're born again. We know we can, because God said to us, "Fear not: for I have redeemed thee, I have called thee by thy name; thou art mine" (Isaiah 43:1).

Notice that's not a suggestion. God didn't say, "Do your best to not fear, but if you can't help it, I'll understand." No, He made it a command. He said, "Fear not!"

He didn't just give us that command once, either. The words *fear not* appear in the Bible 110 times. Add to those such admonitions as "let not your heart be troubled," (John 14:1), and in one way or another the Bible tells us to not fear at least 365 times.

Fear is *not* OK! It's of the devil, and like everything else that's of him, we are to give it no place in our lives (Ephesians 4:27).

"But Brother Copeland, I'm a world-class worrier! I have no idea how to keep fear out of my life."

Maybe not, but you can learn. It's like driving a car. If you've never driven, you wouldn't know how to do that, either. But if you have the physical ability, and I handed you my car keys and told you to drive my car around the block, you could do it. All you'd need is some instruction.

The Victory That Overcomes the World

The same is true when it comes to expelling fear from your life. You have the ability, and God has given you the keys in His WORD. His WORD contains both His instructions and His power, and if you'll agree with it and operate accordingly, you'll be able to do whatever it says. You'll be able to fear not.

It doesn't even matter that, in the natural, such a thing seems impossible to you. It didn't seem possible in the natural for 100-year-old Abraham to have a child with his 90-year-old barren wife, Sarah, either. Yet when God said they would and called Abraham the "father of many nations," Abraham took God at His WORD (Romans 4:17). He decided, *If God said I can father nations, that means I can…* and he did.

You can make that decision where fear is concerned and follow Abraham's example of faith. Make a quality commitment to agree with God, and say, "He commanded me to fear not so, one way or another, I *can* fear not. Therefore, in the Name of Jesus, I refuse to fear. I will fear not!" Once you make that commitment, of course, the question is, how are you going to follow through on it? How do you remain fearless in a world where very real dangers are staring you in the face? How do you stop worrying in a day when problems seem to be piling up in unprecedented numbers, and the news headlines keep warning of more to come? If you're not going to fear, what are you going to do instead?

Answering those questions is what this book is all about.

In every chapter, you'll find out more of what you need to know to deal fearlessly with anything the devil comes up with in these last days. You'll see specifically what God has promised to do for you in the Bible and how to put those promises to work in any situation. You'll read scripture after scripture that assures you that no weapon the devil forms against you can prosper (Isaiah 54:17).

LIVE FEAR FREE

By the time you've finished reading this book, I believe that not only will you be totally unafraid of the devil and his ugly works, he will be fleeing in fear from *you!*

THE LAW OF RECIPROCALS

In fact, with what I'm about to share with you just in the next few pages, you can go ahead and start putting the devil on the run…especially if you're already in a battle with fear right now. You may be under attack in some area of your life and feel like you're losing the fight because you're not sure what God promised to do for you in that area. You may know that in Christ Jesus "all the promises of God…are Yes, and in Him Amen" (2 Corinthians 1:20, *New King James Version),* but you may not yet know what all those promises are.

I was born again at the age of twenty-six when I received Jesus as my Savior and LORD. I needed God's help to straighten out my life, but I didn't know anything about the Bible. I was a scriptural illiterate. Although my parents had taken me to church as a child, I managed to make it through without learning much of The WORD of God at all.

When I began to find out, a few years after I got saved, that the Bible contains my Covenant with God and His exceeding great and precious promises to me, I was thrilled. So, I set about to learn as much as I could as fast as I could.

The more I studied God's WORD, however, the more I realized there was to learn. But thankfully, early in my ministry, The LORD revealed to me a biblical law that accelerated my spiritual progress. What He taught me gave me an edge in overcoming the devil's attacks and the fear that comes with them. It helped me figure out what God would do for me in any devilish situation even before I could find a specific promise about it from His WORD.

The Victory That Overcomes the World

I'll never forget the first time The LORD spoke to me about it. I was sitting in church one Sunday morning and heard Him say in my spirit, *I'm going to teach you the spiritual Bible law of reciprocals.*

Reciprocals? I thought. I was familiar with the word but only as it applied to aviation. Beyond that, I'd never given it any thought. So, after I got home from church, I looked it up in the dictionary.

It said that reciprocals are things that correspond but have been reversed or inverted. North and south, for example, are reciprocals. They correspond. They're both directions on the compass, but they're opposites. One is always at the opposite end of the other. No matter how far north you go, the moment you turn around you're going south. No matter how far south you go, the moment you turn around you're going north.

As I thought about this and applied it to the spiritual realm, I saw what The LORD was trying to get across to me:

Everything the devil does is a reciprocal of what God has done!

The devil never originated anything. He's not a creator. He has no truth in him. All he can do is twist something that originated with God. He can't even create his own lies. He comes up with them by inverting what God said is true.

For example, the devil and the world say *seeing is believing.* But the Bible says *believing is seeing.* It says that we walk by faith, not by sight. The devil and the world say, "Get all the money you can, keep it all, and you'll be rich." But the Bible says, "Give and it will be given to you."

The devil has been twisting God's words into their reciprocals ever since the Garden of Eden. It's how he stole THE BLESSING of God from Adam and Eve. He turned God's WORD around backward. He told Eve that if she and Adam ate of the tree of

LIVE FEAR FREE

the knowledge of good and evil, they would be like God. He convinced her they were forbidden to eat of it because God didn't want them to be like Him (Genesis 3:5).

The truth was just the opposite! God *did* want Adam and Eve to be like Him. He created them in His image. He commanded them to not eat of the tree of the knowledge of good and evil so they could continue to be like Him and not die.

But instead of believing God, Eve believed the devil. She ate of the tree and so did Adam. Afterward, when God came to find them, they hid from Him. He asked them why, and Adam said it was because he was "afraid" (Genesis 3:10).

That was the first time Adam had ever experienced fear. Where did the fear come from? The devil didn't invent it. He produced it by inverting the force of faith that God had put in Adam when He created him.

Fear is the reciprocal of faith! That's the reason fear and faith operate almost exactly alike and produce exactly opposite results.

Once the spiritual law of reciprocals was set in motion through sin, satan used it to twist everything. Under his influence, THE BLESSING became the curse. Love became hate. Health became sickness. Prosperity became poverty. Peace became turmoil. Joy became discouragement, despondency and depression.

How does knowing this law of reciprocals help you? Why does it give you an edge when you're facing a threatening situation, and you need to put fear and the devil underfoot? Because it assures you that God will do for you in that situation the exact opposite of what the devil is doing! It assures you that the very evil with which the devil is threatening you is actually proof that God has a corresponding, but greater BLESSING for you to claim by faith.

The Victory That Overcomes the World

Once you understand this, even if you don't yet know exactly what the Bible says about that situation, you can refute the devil's threats just by turning them around the opposite way!

If finances get tight and satan starts telling you you're not going to have enough, you can say to him, "Devil, the very fact that you're telling me I'm not going to have enough proves that God promised to provide me with more than enough!" If problems start piling up and the devil says there's no way out, you can say, "Devil, you just confirmed to me that there is a way out!"

No matter what kind of difficulty arises, if the devil says, "You lose," you can say, "No, I win!"

Don't just stop there. You can't rely on that one spiritual law, and decide you don't need to know anything else. No, faith comes by hearing, and hearing by The WORD of God (Romans 10:17). So, to keep growing in faith and victory you must keep hearing, reading and meditating on The WORD. Keep growing in your knowledge of it so that you can become fully persuaded of the truth of God's WORD and confidently say to the devil and the trials he brings your way, exactly what Jesus said: "It is written!" (Matthew 4:4).

THE REAL IS ALWAYS MORE POWERFUL THAN THE COUNTERFEIT

"But Brother Copeland, what about 1 Corinthians 10:13? Doesn't it say that rather than always giving us victory over trials and temptations, God sometimes just enables us to bear them?"

No, what it says is this:

There hath no temptation taken you but such as is common to man: but God is faithful, who will not suffer you to be tempted above that ye are able; but will with the

LIVE FEAR FREE

temptation also make a way to escape, that ye may be able to bear it.

If you look up the Greek words in that verse, you'll find it agrees with what we saw in 2 Peter 1:4 about God making a way of escape for us through His exceeding great and precious promises. First Corinthians 10:13 says that no trial is so big you can't overcome it with what God has provided for you. There is no problem the devil devises that can keep you trapped because God's way of escape will make you free every time.

God's ways *always* triumph over satan's because there's no truth in satan. All he can do is pervert truth to produce a counterfeit, and the counterfeit is never as powerful as the real. That's why any time the devil comes at you with fear, you can always overcome it with faith. Fear is the counterfeit. Faith is the real.

You can start right now overcoming the devil by faith in Jesus' Name. Even if you're a brand-new believer and don't yet know anything else in the Bible, you know how to call on the Name of Jesus because that's how you got saved.

His Name can save you from any threatening situation, because when Jesus was raised from the dead, He defeated the devil on your behalf. So when you open your mouth and speak that Name by faith, Jesus Himself will back it with His power, and the devil will have to turn tail and run.

I know any number of believers, me included, who have proven this time and again. I could fill an entire book with their testimonies.

I'm remembering right now, for example, a pastor I knew years ago who lived in Los Angeles. He was walking home from church one night after a service when a group of men started following along behind him. Sensing something was wrong, he

The Victory That Overcomes the World

started running to get away from them, but they caught him and started beating him.

He managed to break free long enough to make it to the porch of a nearby house where some of his church members lived and began banging on the door. The church members opened it a little but then they saw the gang of men coming after him and shut it again. They didn't want that wild bunch to get into their house!

Grabbing a broom he found on the porch, the pastor swung it at the attackers. In response, one of the young men pulled a weapon.

This pastor is a man of God. He was no spiritual novice. But until then, he'd just been reacting in the natural. When he saw the gravity of the situation, however, he realized he needed supernatural help. So, he hollered, "In the Name of The LORD Jesus Christ of Nazareth, you touch not God's anointed and do him no harm!" (See 1 Chronicles 16:22.)

At those words, the attackers backed up. When they did, the pastor pointed his finger at them and hollered again, "In the Name of Jesus," and they backed up some more. The third time he hollered that Name, they turned around and ran off.

On his way home, the pastor thought, *Why didn't I do that sooner?*

Good question!

The Name of Jesus would have worked before that gang ever landed a blow. It would have worked before they even got close.

Faith in Jesus' Name will work for any believer in any situation. It will work for you even if all you know is that, according to the law of reciprocals, whenever satan launches an attack, God

LIVE FEAR FREE

always has something much greater that will overcome it. It will work for you even if all you know to say, is, "In Jesus' Name, get'em, God!"

One young woman I know of was delivered from an extremely dangerous situation by saying something almost that simple. She had been attending some meetings where I had been preaching these things. One morning, as she was getting ready to come to the service, an intruder got into her house. She didn't know the man was there until suddenly he got into the shower with her.

As she told Gloria later, the intruder got his arm around her head. For a second, panic flew all over her. Then she remembered what I had preached the day before and shouted as loud as she could, "In the Name of Jesus, you turn me loose!" Sure enough, the intruder let go of her and backed out of the shower.

She followed him and kept repeating, "In the Name of Jesus." Every time she said it, the man backed up a little farther until, finally, she had backed him all the way into the living room, into his trousers, and out the front door.

Once he was gone, she finished getting ready and came to the meeting!

START PRACTICING NOW

I think the most astounding testimony I've ever heard along these lines, though, is that of a man named Norman Williams. He experienced God's miraculous delivering power in the midst of one of the worst aviation disasters in history. Although I never met him, I read his account of it; and as a pilot, I am very familiar with the details of that disaster.

It happened on a foggy day in 1977 on a runway in the Canary Islands. An 800,000-pound KLM 747 airliner that had

The Victory That Overcomes the World

just topped off its fuel ran broadside into a Pan American 747. The collision burst the forward tanks of the KLM, dumped jet fuel into the cabin of the Pan American, and ignited an inferno so intense that witnesses later reported seeing people's flesh melt and fall off their bones.

Ultimately, more than 550 people died in the catastrophe. And Norman Williams, a born-again middle-aged businessman, was right in the middle of it. What saved him? The same thing that saved the pastor in Los Angeles and the young woman in Honolulu. When he saw what was happening, he shouted in the face of what looked like hell itself, "I'M STANDING ON THE WORD! IN THE NAME OF JESUS, BY THE BLOOD OF THE LAMB!"

As he recounts in his book, *Terror at Tenerife,* the moment he said those words, all fear left him. When he hollered them again, an invisible force got him up out of his seat and into the aisle of the plane. He could see a white-hot ball of fire coming toward him, but somehow it never hit him. Instead, as he kept shouting, "I'm standing on The WORD! In the Name of Jesus, by the blood of the Lamb!" the unseen force kept moving him until, looking up, he saw a hole in the ceiling right above him. It looked like a way of escape, but he didn't know how to reach it.

The distance from the floor to the ceiling of a 747 is a good ten feet. No way could a man, who by his own admission weighed 250 pounds and was totally out of shape, jump that high. But Norman kept shouting about The WORD, the Name, and the blood of Jesus, and the next thing he knew, his head was sticking up out of that hole. He shouted again and made it all the way through the hole. He ran down the wing of the airplane, jumped off the end of it onto the runway thirty feet below, and made it to safety.

LIVE FEAR FREE

He had shrapnel from the molten metal embedded in his skin, but in the hospital the next morning when he woke up, he found little pieces of molten metal all over his pillow. They had come out of his flesh during the night while he was sleeping, without him even knowing it.

What happened in that situation?

Norman Williams chose faith instead of fear, and the Spirit of God got involved! The angels of The LORD got involved! Just as the Fourth Man showed up in the fiery furnace to protect and deliver Shadrach, Meshach and Abednego when the king threw them into the fiery furnace (Daniel 3), the Fourth Man showed up at Tenerife to deliver Norman Williams.

"But Brother Copeland, I'm not sure I could do what Mr. Williams did that day."

Sure you could. If you're born again, you have the same right to the Name of Jesus and the blood of the Lamb that he has. You also have the same capacity to fear not.

I don't recommend waiting until you're in a burning airplane to develop that capacity, though. I recommend you start practicing now, because in times of crisis it's what you do every day that kicks in. When you're suddenly facing a perilous situation, your brain shuts down and your spirit takes over. You just automatically say what's in your heart in abundance, for out of the abundance of the heart the mouth speaks (Luke 6:45).

So, renew your mind to the spiritual law of reciprocals and keep feeding your spirit on God's WORD. Study what you're about to read in this book. Get it down inside you, until it becomes a revelation to you that you don't have to fear anything the devil does in these perilous last days.

The Victory That Overcomes the World

He's not really the hotshot he claims to be. You're the one with the Name of Jesus and the faith that overcomes the world. You can beat the devil *every time.*

CHAPTER 2

THE LAW OF THE SPIRIT OF LIFE IN CHRIST JESUS

CHAPTER 2

THE LAW OF THE SPIRIT OF LIFE IN CHRIST JESUS

The LORD is on my side: I will not fear. (Psalm 118:6)

THE WORDS *I WILL* ARE among the strongest in the English language. When you say, "I will not fear," you're saying you have made a quality decision about which there is no debate and from which there is no turning back. You're declaring, "For me, it will be this way and no other: Regardless of what happens around me or what other people may choose to do, I refuse to fear."

That's a bold declaration. Yet, as a believer, you can make it with confidence. You can commit to living a fear-free life for the same reason the psalmist could: because The LORD is on your side!

He is so thoroughly on your side that He made you His very own child.

He is so committed to BLESSING you that He sent Jesus to shed His precious blood to redeem you, spirit, soul and body, from every work of the devil.

LIVE FEAR FREE

He loves you so much that He paid the highest price ever paid for anything, to reverse what satan did in Adam so that you could be born again from death to life.

God is so totally for you and me, and all believers, that even before we called on Him for salvation, He provided it for us. And as Romans 8:31-32 says, "If God be for us, who can be against us? He that spared not his own Son, but delivered him up for us all, how shall he not with him also freely give us all things?"

Think about it! This is the Creator of the heavens and the earth we're talking about. This is the Almighty One, the Most High—the One for whom nothing is impossible. With Him on our side, no one can stand against us. Nothing can overcome us. With The LORD on our side, we have no reason to fear and every reason not to!

In fact, fear doesn't even come naturally to us as believers. It's foreign to our spirits because when we received Jesus as our LORD, we received a new spiritual nature. Our old sin-and-fear-infested nature died, and we received the nature of Christ. In Him, we have become "a new creature: old things are passed away; behold, all things are become new. And all things are of God" (2 Corinthians 5:17-18).

In other words, all the same qualities, forces and characteristics of God are now in us that were originally in Adam. And as we saw in Chapter 1, Adam didn't have any fear in him when God first made him. He was a faith man created in God's image.

As God's born-again child, the same is true of you. You are a faith being! Your reborn spirit doesn't produce fear. It's no longer a natural force for you. You have been re-created in God's image, and you did not receive from Him "the spirit of bondage again to fear, but you received the Spirit of adoption by whom we cry out, 'Abba, Father'" (Romans 8:15, *New King James Version*).

The Law of the Spirit of Life in Christ Jesus

Fear might still seem to come naturally to you, but that's only because you've been practicing it. You have continued to give place to it the same way you used to before you were born again. Back then, fear actually was natural for you because your spirit was still producing the reciprocal of God's WORD. That's not the case anymore. But if you allow fear to get into you from the outside, your spirit can house it, even though your reborn human spirit doesn't produce it anymore. It produces faith.

Faith is what enables you to cry out to God, "Abba, Father!" *Abba* means "Daddy." It's a term of belonging. It's different than the word *Father*. Even people who have no personal relationship with God call Him Father. But they don't say it with faith, confident that He loves them and is on their side. They say it as if He's someone to be afraid of, as if they're backing away from Him in fear of what He might do to them.

Those of us who know God as *Abba* don't have to back away from Him. We can run *to* Him. We can have the same attitude natural children have when, seeing their father holding an ice cream cone or some other treat, they run to him saying, "Daddy, Daddy! I want some of that!" The very word *daddy* reveals how much faith the child has in his or her father. It indicates that child already knows Daddy is going to give them what they ask.

I was like that with my mother whenever she was cooking. As a young boy, I would follow her around the kitchen sticking my fingers into whatever she was making so I could get a taste of it. Sometimes she got aggravated at me being underfoot and tried to shoo me away. But I stayed right there, looking up at her (and as I grew taller, looking over her shoulder) saying, "I want some of that."

What made me so bold?

LIVE FEAR FREE

She is my momma! I'm her boy, and I know she loves me. It would have never occurred to me to crawl into her kitchen on my knees and beg her to give me a taste of something. I would never have said to her, "Mother, I'm so unworthy. Could I just have the crumbs?"

There would have been no faith in that—only fear. Yet, Christians can often be heard saying exactly those kinds of things to God. They'll pray, "Oh, Father, if I could just have the crumbs off Your table, that will be enough."

The Bible doesn't say anything about us eating crumbs off God's table, or His floor. It says He prepares a table before us in the presence of our enemies (Psalm 23:5). Our enemies are the devil and his bunch. They're the ones who have to be afraid of God, not us. We're God's beloved children. Instead of groveling on the floor in fear, we ought to leave the floor-groveling to the devil. We ought to say to him, "Hey, enemy, if you're going to hang around underneath God's table, stay off my feet, because I'm scooting up to the table and eating the feast my Daddy has prepared for me!"

"But Brother Copeland, aren't there verses in the Bible that say we are to fear The LORD?"

Yes, but the word translated *fear* in those scriptures actually means "to honor and reverence." There's a big difference between reverencing someone and being frightened of them. Matthew 15:4 *(New King James Version),* for example says, "Honor your father and your mother," but it's not telling children to be frightened of their parents.

If a child is afraid of his or her parents, there's something wrong. When the relationship between them is healthy, the child has faith in his parents' love, so he is never afraid of them. Yet he also honors and respects them enough to obey them.

The Law of the Spirit of Life in Christ Jesus

That's the kind of relationship I had with my natural father, A.W. Copeland. I called him "Daddy" all the days of his life. I didn't care whether it sounded mature or not. He was my buddy. But growing up, I also knew that, as my father, he would whip me good if I lied, sassed my mother, or did something else that was seriously wrong.

Proverbs 13:24 says, "He who spares his rod hates his son, but he who loves him disciplines him promptly" *(New King James Version)*. And my daddy loved me, so, when I needed stern discipline, there was an occasional manifestation of the rod. I wasn't too happy about that as a youngster. But as an adult, I was grateful for it and taught my own children that kind of honor and respect. I made sure they understood I was both their *daddy* and their *father*.

For instance, when John was a little boy and he heard me say, "I told you thirty minutes ago to get in bed, and you'd better get in there now!" he knew that was Father speaking. He wasn't afraid of me. He knew I loved him and that, as his daddy, I'm his buddy. But he also had enough reverence and honor for me as his father to know he'd better mind me. He'd learned that I'm true to my word, and I don't lie to him. If I said I would spank him for misbehaving, I would do what I said.

That's how it is for us, as believers, in our relationship with God. We honor and reverence Him as our Father and, at the same time, we know that He loves us and that He's our Abba, our Daddy. We can boldly say, "The LORD is on my side: I will not fear!" because we are born of Him, and He has not given us a spirit of fear but a spirit of faith.

POWERFUL SPIRITUAL FORCES

Faith is God's creative power. It's the spiritual force He uses to bring His WORD to pass. Anytime it's in operation, you're going to come out better. Faith will always do you good.

As faith's reciprocal, fear does the exact opposite. It will always do damage. Anytime it's in operation, it's going to make things worse because it is the spiritual force satan uses to bring his evil will to pass. It's not just an intellectual concept or an emotional feeling. It's actually a negative spiritual force.

Have you ever noticed when someone is badly startled, they're likely to put their hand on their chest and say something like, "That scared me so much it made my heart come right up in my throat"? Without realizing it, they're correctly identifying where the fear came from. It came from their heart, or their spirit.

It may not have been produced by their spirit. In fact, as we've already seen, if they're believers, it definitely wasn't. Born-again human spirits don't produce fear. For it to get inside us, we must allow it to get in from the outside by entertaining and accepting it.

What would cause us to do that? To quote Hosea 4:6 again, a "lack of knowledge."

Most Christians unintentionally let fear get into their spirits because they don't know any better. Most of the time, they aren't even aware that they've done it. When they encounter a threatening situation and fear comes up out of their spirits, they just assume it showed up in response to the situation. But it didn't. The fear came up because it was already in them. Somewhere along the line, they allowed it to get back into their spirits and, at that moment, it came out.

We all have had this experience. We've inadvertently let fear

The Law of the Spirit of Life in Christ Jesus

enter into us at times and had it working in us without being aware of it.

"Well," someone might say, "I know how fear feels, so wouldn't I be aware of it if it were inside me?"

Not necessarily, because fear is not a feeling. It's a spiritual force.

Spiritual forces can function without you feeling them. Think about the spiritual force of faith and you'll realize that's true. You can't tell if you have faith or if it is working in you by checking your natural feelings.

Faith doesn't have anything to do with feelings. It functions in the spirit. It goes to work in you when you plant the spiritual seed of God's WORD in your heart. If you keep The WORD in your heart and mouth and don't allow the devil to steal it, the spiritual force of faith will keep working in and for you until that WORD becomes a manifest reality in your life. As Jesus said in Mark 4:

> So is the kingdom of God, as if a man should cast seed into the ground; and should sleep, and rise night and day, and the seed should spring and grow up, he knoweth not how. For the earth bringeth forth fruit of herself; first the blade, then the ear, after that the full corn in the ear (verses 26-28).

Notice, Jesus didn't say the man got up in the middle of the night and dug up his seed to check on it because he couldn't feel it growing. No, the man knew his feelings didn't have anything to do with it. He understood that once in the ground, the seed would do what it was designed to do. Down in the soil, where he couldn't see or feel it happening, the growth process would take place, and he'd eventually get a crop.

That's how it is with faith in God's WORD. It works unseen

LIVE FEAR FREE

and unfelt in the human heart just as that man's seed did in the soil. The same is true of fear. Because it's a spiritual force it, too, can be working in us without our being able to feel it. Just as faith can be working unseen and unfelt in a believer to produce healing, fear can be working in someone without them feeling it, to make them sick.

Even medical science confirms that fear can and does produce diseases such as arthritis, heart disease, digestive problems, immune disorders and a host of other maladies. Fear can cripple the human mind, change the color of a person's hair, and even blind their eyes. I've talked to doctors who told me that 80 percent or more of the patients in hospitals are there because of fear, anxiety and worry.

Worry is so common that many people don't even think of it as fear, but it is. It's meditating on a lie of the devil until it scares you. Worry will cause you to call negative things that don't yet exist into existence. It will cause you to bathe yourself in fear until you speak of what you're worried about as if it had already happened and, as a result, it sometimes will. Even if it doesn't happen, the worry itself will damage your body.

That's why it's not unusual to hear people say things like, "I just worried myself sick." That's literally what they did.

DIFFERENT LAWS, DIFFERENT RESULTS

Why are worry and fear so consistently destructive?

Because they activate the operation of the spiritual *law of sin and death*.

That law is the most hellish spiritual law ever set in motion on this earth. It's the satanic reciprocal of the spiritual master law originally established by God, *the law of life*.

The Law of the Spirit of Life in Christ Jesus

If you're not familiar with the concept of spiritual laws, they govern the operations of the spirit realm much like the laws of physics govern the natural world. So, where God's law of life produced nothing but BLESSING and good on the earth, when the law of sin and death went into operation, it began producing the opposite. It perverted the law of life and brought forth all the deadly manifestations of the curse. It became the evil master law of the spirit realm and began its cruel reign over mankind.

The law of sin and death is still in operation today. It is still as deadly as ever, but—thanks be to God—you don't have to let it reign over you. You can reign over it instead, because through the plan of Redemption God has established another spiritual master law. One that is not only greater than the law of sin and death, but is higher and even more powerful than the original law of the spirit of life.

What is this higher law?

The law of the Spirit of life in Christ Jesus!

The law of the Spirit of life in Christ Jesus is the law that went into operation in your life when you were born again. It's the law that enabled you to be delivered out of the kingdom of darkness and into the kingdom of God's dear Son. The law that liberated you from the curse so that even in a world where the curse is still in operation, you can enjoy the Life and BLESSING of God.

The Apostle Paul wrote: "The law of the Spirit of life in Christ Jesus hath made me free from the law of sin and death" (Romans 8:2)! That's true of every believer. Yet not every believer is walking in that freedom on a day-to-day basis. Many are still suffering needlessly under the effects of the law of sin and death.

Why? Once again, it's because of a lack of knowledge. It's because they haven't learned enough about those two laws to

LIVE FEAR FREE

distinguish between them. They don't have a clear understanding of how each one manifests in various areas of life.

As a result, they can get confused as to which law is behind whatever might be happening to them. They can fail to recognize that the law of sin and death is trying to operate illegally in their lives and wind up accepting rather than rejecting its manifestations. They might even mistake those manifestations as coming from the law of the Spirit of life.

I've seen Christians make this mistake time and again. I've heard precious, sincere believers claim, for example, that a little fear is actually healthy. I've heard them say things like God sometimes puts sickness on us to teach us something, that it can actually be "a BLESSING in disguise."

Falling prey to such confusion is always dangerous. And because it makes you an easy target for the devil, it can be especially costly in these last days. So, I want to spend the rest of this chapter and the next immunizing you against it. I want to help you get clearly established in your mind the basic scriptural facts about the law of sin and death and the law of the Spirit of life in Christ Jesus.

Once you're equipped with this knowledge, you'll easily be able to identify which law is trying to operate in your life. You'll be able to determine instantly what you should accept and embrace as a BLESSING of God and what to reject as an effect of the curse. And neither the devil nor anyone else will ever be able to confuse you about it again.

The first question we need to answer is this:

Who is the Spirit of life?

The answer is: *The Holy Spirit.* He is the Life Giver.

The Law of the Spirit of Life in Christ Jesus

The second question is: *Where does the law of the Spirit of life operate?*

The answer is: *It operates in Christ Jesus.*

Does anything of satan operate in Christ Jesus?

No. Jesus Himself said in John 14:30, "the prince of this world" (satan) "…hath nothing in me."

That means the law of the Spirit of life in Christ Jesus has absolutely nothing in common with the law of sin and death. None of the things that came into the world through satan—such as sin, sickness, disease or lack—can be found in Jesus, and there's no part of Jesus in satan. They are entirely separate from one another, and the laws by which they operate produce entirely different results.

What results does the master law of the Spirit of life in Christ Jesus produce?

If we were to put them in order, number one on the list would be the new birth. That's the first thing you received when you believed on Jesus. The instant the law of the Spirit of life went into operation, eternal life was imparted to you, and you were born again.

The next result on our list could be the Baptism in the Holy Spirit. The Bible says when the Holy Spirit comes on you, you receive "power" and "where the Spirit of The LORD is, there is liberty (emancipation from bondage, freedom)" (Acts 1:8; 2 Corinthians 3:17, *Amplified Bible, Classic Edition)*. So, clearly those things are produced by the law of the Spirit of life.

We could also include healing and deliverance from demonic oppression on the list because Acts 10:38 says, "God anointed Jesus of Nazareth with the Holy Ghost and with power: who

LIVE FEAR FREE

went about doing good, and healing all that were oppressed of the devil...."

Those are just a few of the results produced by this powerful master law. There are many more, but if we were to write down those we've mentioned, the list would look like this:

The Master Law of the Spirit of Life in Christ Jesus

- The new birth
- The Baptism in the Holy Spirit
- Healing
- Deliverance from demonic oppression

Every one of those things works by spiritual law. None of them happens just by accident. The new birth didn't just randomly fall on you one day. You received it when you activated the law of the Spirit of life in Christ Jesus by receiving Him as your LORD and Savior.

At the time you did it, you probably didn't even realize you'd activated that law. My wife, Gloria, certainly didn't. When she received Jesus as her LORD and was born again shortly after we married, she had no idea spiritual law even existed. She'd never even heard of the new birth. She just picked up the Bible my mother had given me for my birthday and saw that inside it, my mother had written, "Ken, precious. Happy birthday, today. Seek ye first the kingdom of God and all these things will be added to you. Matthew 6:33."

Reading that inscription, Gloria thought about all the things we needed to have added to us. (We had almost nothing back then, so we needed everything!) So, she looked up the verse. After reading the verses around it, she prayed: "LORD, I'm just giving You my life. Take my life and do something with it." Unknowingly, she activated the law of the Spirit of life in Christ Jesus and got born again.

Two weeks later, I did too. Sitting in our little apartment, I heard The LORD say, *Kenneth, if you don't get right with Me you are headed for a devil's hell.* I knew it was true, and I was ready to get right with Him. I just didn't know how. *What should I do?* I thought.

Instantly, inside me I heard the voice of my boyhood Sunday school teacher, Mrs. Taggart, saying what, as a youngster, I'd heard her say so often. "Boys, you need to ask Jesus to come into your heart." I thought, *That's Old Lady Taggart!* (That's how she used to refer to herself.)

The idea of asking Jesus to come into my heart still sounded as dumb to me as it had thirteen years before when I was twelve. But I did it anyway. And I was changed forever.

Mrs. Taggart won me to The LORD years after she went to heaven! What made that possible? The seed of God's WORD she had sown into my life was still in me. It had never sprouted because I had never done anything about it. But on that November day in 1962, when I believed and acted on that WORD, the law of the Spirit of life in Christ Jesus went into operation. It made me free from the law of sin and death, and I was born again.

GOD'S LAWS NEVER CHANGE

How we receive the new birth is how we receive everything God has promised and provided for us. It's how we live fear free and victoriously on a day-to-day basis. We activate the Spirit of the law of life in Christ Jesus by believing and acting on God's WORD.

LIVE FEAR FREE

The law of the Spirit of life in Christ Jesus will work for you in any situation. Just as it made you a new creation in Christ through the new birth, it will free you from fear, heal your body, and deliver you from lack. It will overcome the law of sin and death in any area of your life.

Christians who don't understand this often continue to struggle with worry and anxiety because they feel like victims of circumstance. When they're faced with a bad situation, all they know to do is pray and beg God to move on their behalf, and then accept whatever happens. Sometimes, their prayers get answered, but they don't realize it was because they accidentally slipped over into faith and activated spiritual law.

As a result, some very strange ideas have gotten into the Body of Christ. People have had "faith accidents" and come up with their own explanations for them. Some Sunday morning at church a sick person might suddenly get healed, for example, and run around the church shouting for joy. Not knowing the person was responding in faith to a healing scripture they saw in the Bible, the congregation might assume the healing took place because the person ran and shouted. They might start *The Shout, Run and Be Healed* denomination and tell everyone, "That's the way God is moving in these last days."

When not everyone who runs and shouts gets healed, they might decide that God heals some people and not others. They might start telling people that everyone should shout and run, but not everyone will get healed because healing is not always God's will.

Talk about an unscriptural idea! Nowhere in the New Testament does it say that Jesus is going around picking who He wants to heal. According to the Gospels, He healed all who came to Him when He was on earth, and He hasn't changed. He has

The Law of the Spirit of Life in Christ Jesus

made healing available to everyone. Anyone, anytime, anywhere can receive healing through the law of the Spirit of life in Christ Jesus by believing and acting on God's WORD.

God's spiritual laws always work! You don't even have to understand why in order to benefit from them. You can just put them into operation by faith and enjoy the results.

You do this all the time with the laws of physics. If you want to travel rapidly across the country, you just buy a ticket and get on a jet airliner. You don't have to know anything about aerodynamics or jet engines. You just have to know the plane will fly and that it will take you where you want to go. And you trust that the pilot and crew are qualified to operate it.

God is qualified to operate the laws of the Spirit! He knows everything about them. All we need is to trust Him and do what He says.

When I first started doing that, I didn't understand much of anything about God's laws. In fact, some of the things He said in the Bible didn't make much mental sense to me at all. But even so, they produced great BLESSING in my life because I went ahead and acted on them by faith.

Faith always works. Like the law of the Spirit of life in Christ Jesus, it's one of God's spiritual laws (Romans 3:27), and His laws never fail or change. People might think they do because they don't know what the Bible says, but then they might think that about some of the laws of physics, too, if they don't know any better.

In 1903, for instance, when the Wright brothers flew their first airplane, some people might have thought the law of gravity had changed, but it hadn't. The Wright brothers had just learned more about how to work with that law. They'd figured out how

37

LIVE FEAR FREE

to supersede it with the law of lift. Airplanes would have flown in 1803 just as surely as they did a hundred years later. The laws have always been there. They have never changed.

That's how it is with the law of the Spirit of life in Christ Jesus. It has never changed. It can't change because Jesus doesn't change.

He is "the same yesterday, and to day, and for ever" (Hebrews 13:8).

So is your heavenly Father.

He said, "I am The LORD, I change not" (Malachi 3:6). He is, and always will be, your Abba, Father...which means you can boldly say today and forever, "I will not fear; The LORD is on my side!"

CHAPTER 3

FOCUS ON THE WORD, NOT THE WAVES

CHAPTER 3

FOCUS ON THE WORD, NOT THE WAVES

For the thing which I greatly feared is come upon me,
and that which I was afraid of is come unto me.
(Job 3:25)

NOW THAT WE'VE EXAMINED THE law of the Spirit of life in Christ Jesus, let's look further at its reciprocal, the law of sin and death. That law, although it no longer reigns supreme, is important for us to understand because we need to know how to be on guard against it. If we don't, even though we're born again, we can still fall prey to some of its effects.

So, let's go over the basic facts about it. Let's ask and answer the same questions about the law of sin and death we did in Chapter 2 about the law of the Spirit of life in Christ Jesus. As before, the number one question is this:

Who is the spirit of sin and death?

The answer is *satan*. He is the author of all sin and "the thief" who comes to steal and kill and destroy (John 10:10).

Question two: *Where does the law of sin and death operate?*

It operates in and through satan wherever anyone either knowingly or unknowingly cooperates with him by believing his lies.

LIVE FEAR FREE

Question three: *Is there anything of Christ Jesus in satan?*

No. Jesus said about Himself, "I am the truth" (John 14:6) and He said about the devil, "There is no truth in him" (John 8:44). Jesus has no part with the works of satan, and satan has no part in the works of Jesus.

I said this before, but it bears repeating: Jesus and satan are entirely separate. So are their laws. The dividing line between them is clear. It has only been crossed once—and that was when Jesus subjected Himself to the law of sin and death as our Substitute so we could be set free from it.

Question four: *What are the results of the law of sin and death?*

The polar opposite of those produced by the law of the Spirit of life in Christ Jesus. For instance, the law of the Spirit of life in Christ Jesus makes us the righteousness of God (2 Corinthians 5:21). The law of sin and death never made anyone righteous, and never will. The law of the Spirit of life in Christ Jesus provides us with healing. The devil never healed anyone, and he never will.

As obvious as this may seem, I've known people to get confused about it. I've actually heard it said that if satan can make you sick, he can also heal you. That's ridiculous. The devil's very presence emanates sickness. He *is* sick. He's spiritually sick. He wishes he could make you well and get the credit for it, but he can't. There's a fire burning on the inside of him that's consuming him, and there's nothing he can do about it.

If we were to list some of the results the law of sin and death produces, we could include such things as:

- Spiritual death
- Sickness and disease

Focus on The WORD, Not the Waves

- Poverty and lack
- Grief and sorrow
- Failure and loss.

All those things operate according to spiritual law. And as we've already seen, for spiritual laws to operate, they must be put into motion. What's different about the law of sin and death, however, is that the whole world is going with its negative flow. So, if you're not watchful, you'll slip into that flow, and its results will automatically overtake you.

Why is that? Because unlike God who respects your free will, satan is a dominator. He is also a deceiver. Since he can't put any of his trash on you without your consent, he tries to trick you into giving your consent without realizing it by getting you to yield to fear.

Just as faith is the spiritual force that sets in motion the law of the Spirit of life in Christ Jesus, fear sets in motion the law of sin and death and brings its results into manifestation. One place we see this borne out in the Bible is in the book of Job. There, Job said it himself, as he was mourning over all the tragedy and loss he had experienced: "The thing I greatly feared is come upon me" (Job 3:25).

"But Brother Copeland, I thought God was behind all the bad stuff that happened to Job."

Then you need to go back and read the book of Job again. The very first chapter makes it clear that God didn't have anything to do with all the destruction that descended on Job. The devil was behind it all. He hated the man because he was upright. He also resented the protective hedge God had put around him. So he said to God, "Put forth thine hand now, and touch all that he hath, and he will curse thee to thy face."

43

LIVE FEAR FREE

God, however, wouldn't do it. He said to satan, "Behold, all that he hath is in thy power; only upon himself put not forth thine hand" (Job 1:11–12).

God didn't say that to cause trouble for Job. He said it because He's honest, and it was the truth. Through fear, Job had gotten over into satan's territory. Once satan knew this, he almost destroyed the man. He set about to pressure Job into cursing God and dying. But Job refused to do either one. He never cursed God, and he didn't die because where those two things were concerned, he stayed in faith.

KEEP THE THERMOSTAT CONNECTED TO THE FURNACE

I've said it before, but it bears repeating: Faith will stop the devil every time! Even in a world that's being swept downstream toward destruction on the current of the law of sin and death, faith will propel you upstream into the BLESSINGS of God. Instead of bringing upon you the things you greatly fear, faith will bring into your life the good and desirable things God has promised you. For as Hebrews 11:1 says, "Faith is the substance of things hoped for, the evidence of things not seen."

Notice, according to that scripture, hope alone won't get the job done. For God's promises to become a manifest reality in our lives, hope and faith must work together. I like how Charles Capps used to explain this. He compared hope and faith to a thermostat and a furnace. Like a thermostat, hope sets the desired goal, but it doesn't have any power on its own to make that goal a reality. The power comes from faith. So, for the two to work properly they must be connected.

If we don't realize this, we can wind up like old Backwoods Joe who lived in a shack out in the woods. One cold day, he went to visit his friend and was intrigued when he saw the friend walk over to the thermostat and turn up the temperature. Feeling the heat come on, Joe pointed to the gadget on the wall and said to his friend, "What is that thing?"

"A thermostat," replied the friend.

"Where can I get one?"

"The hardware store, I guess."

Thrilled over this new discovery, Joe went down to the hardware store and bought a thermostat. He took it out to his shack, nailed it to the wall, and set it to seventy degrees. Then he sat back with a big smile on his face and waited for it to warm up the room.

After a while of sitting there in the cold, he started thinking, *I guess God just doesn't want me warm. I guess thermostats just don't work for me.*

He was wrong, of course. God wasn't the problem, and neither was the thermostat. The problem was Joe didn't have the whole operation going.

As believers, we've sometimes had the same problem. We've set our hope on what God has promised us without putting the rest of the system into operation by firing up the furnace of faith.

What exactly is the furnace of faith? It's your heart! Faith comes out of the heart. And since "faith *cometh* by hearing, and hearing by The WORD of God" (Romans 10:17), for faith to come out of your heart you must first put The WORD into it. The WORD powers up your faith like electricity or natural gas powers up a furnace. It's faith fuel!

In the natural, no matter how good a furnace you have, if you

LIVE FEAR FREE

try to fuel it with some alien substance, you're not going to get any heat out of it. Likewise, even though as a born-again believer you have a good heart, if you keep feeding fear into it you're not going to get any faith-power out of it.

This is why satan has worked so hard to convince you and everyone else in the world that fear is normal. That's why he's done everything he can to weave fear into our vocabulary. He wants to get us to where we talk fear all the time, without even noticing it.

Just listen to people talk and you'll see how well he's succeeded. Ask someone, for example, if they're planning to attend a special meeting at church. They're likely to say something like, "No, I'm afraid I'm just too busy to make it."

Why couldn't they just say they were busy? Why did they have to mention being *afraid?* They didn't. It's just a habit they picked up from living in a world that's been schooled in fear by the devil.

Listen to parents talking to their children and you're likely to hear something similar. Parents taking their child out to play might say, "Sweetheart, don't run into the street. We're afraid you'll get run over by a car." Why did they put *we're afraid* in there? Because they think that fear will protect their child.

"But Brother Copeland, don't children need to have a fear of cars to learn not to play in the street?"

No, the fear of being killed by a car will actually put them in greater danger.

Children can learn to stay out of the street without fear being instilled in them. All it takes is a little training and information about how to stay safe around automobiles. Add to that some teaching from The WORD, and the child will be doubly protected. Instill in him scriptural promises such as those in Psalm 91. Then, if he encounters a dangerous situation due to

46

Focus on The WORD, Not the Waves

someone else being careless with an automobile, he'll be able to respond in faith and not in fear.

FEAR TOLERATED IS FAITH CONTAMINATED

Fear and faith don't mix. Fear tolerated is faith contaminated!

We can see in Mark 4 how Jesus' first twelve disciples allowed their faith to be contaminated with fear, even after they'd spent practically the entire day listening to Him teach The WORD. He had told them in detail how faith comes by hearing The WORD of God, how to guard it, and how to operate in it. In a private session with them where He "explained everything [fully]" (verse 34, *Amplified Bible, Classic Edition),* He specifically warned them about what happens to people who hear The WORD and then yield to fear. "The cares and anxieties of the world…creep in and choke and suffocate The WORD, and it becomes fruitless," He said (verse 19, *Amplified Bible, Classic Edition).*

Apparently, however, what He taught them didn't stick with them very long, because—

The same day, when the even was come, he saith unto them, Let us pass over unto the other side [of the lake]. And when they had sent away the multitude, they took him even as he was in the ship. And there were also with him other little ships. And there arose a great storm of wind, and the waves beat into the ship, so that it was now full. And he was in the hinder part of the ship, asleep on a pillow: and they awake him, and say unto him, Master, carest thou not that we perish? (verses 35-38).

What happened there? The disciples yielded to fear, and it contaminated their faith.

47

LIVE FEAR FREE

With all The WORD they'd heard that day, their faith should have been roaring! They should have received as The WORD of The LORD what Jesus said to them right before they got into the boat. Their attitude should have been, *The Master said we're going to the other side of the lake, and come what may, that's what we're going to do!*

The storm shouldn't have surprised them. Jesus had already told them that "satan cometh immediately" to steal The WORD when it's sown in people's hearts (Mark 4:15). And that's exactly what happened. The devil immediately whipped up the wind to make it look like The WORD wasn't going to come to pass. He tricked the disciples into letting fear take them over to the point that they told Jesus, "We're dying!"

Jesus didn't say anything to them about dying. He didn't say, "Let's go to the middle of the lake, sink and die." He said, "We are going to the other side." But instead of believing His WORD, the disciples believed the contrary evidence provided by the windstorm. They became so frightened that they actually accused Jesus of going to sleep because He didn't care about them.

Certainly He cared about them! But He also knew the power of His WORD. So, having delivered it to them, He expected His disciples to believe and act on it. He trusted them with His WORD and went to the back of the boat and went to sleep.

He'll do the same in your life. He'll give you His WORD and just expect you to believe it. He won't jump up and take over every time a storm hits. He'll wait for you to deal with the storm by faith in His WORD.

Why? Because He has more confidence in The WORD and more confidence in you than you do. He knows who you are. You're a born-again, Spirit-filled warrior of the gospel! You don't

Focus on The WORD, Not the Waves

have any business cowering in the face of trouble. You don't have any business yielding to worry and fear and saying things like, "Why doesn't God help me? Doesn't He care?" Your job is to stand strong in faith and declare God's WORD.

That's what Jesus intended for His disciples to do that night on the lake. He fully intended for them to stand up on the bow of the boat and say to the storm, "The Son of the living God told us we're going to the other side of this lake, and we're going if we have to walk. So, peace, be still!"

What would have happened if they'd done that? The storm would have obeyed them just like it obeyed Jesus. Then, they could have awakened Jesus and told Him all about it, and He could have put His arm around them and said, "Well done, faithful servants!"

That would have been great. But it's not the way things went. Instead of commending the disciples, Jesus did what they should have done. "He arose, and rebuked the wind, and said unto the sea, Peace, be still. And the wind ceased, and there was a great calm. And he said unto them, Why are ye so fearful? How is it that ye have no faith?" (verses 39-40).

Those questions clearly indicate the disciples had the opportunity to choose faith over fear in that situation. We, as believers, have the same opportunity. Especially in these last days, we have more access to The WORD of God than any previous generation.

We have multiple versions of the Bible available to us in print. We have Bibles in digital form on our computers, laptops and electronic notebooks. We can even download the Bible onto our phone and carry it around with us wherever we go. Not only can we hear The WORD preached at church, we can hear it preached on television and the internet twenty-four hours a day.

LIVE FEAR FREE

Sure, we live in perilous times. But so what? We're equipped for them. If we let them scare us, Jesus could very well say to us the same thing He said to those first twelve disciples:

"Why are ye so fearful? How is it that ye have no faith?"

DON'T WAIT FOR A CRISIS TO DEVELOP YOUR MEASURE OF FAITH

"But Brother Copeland," someone might say, "I've prayed and prayed for God to give me more faith. He just hasn't done it yet."

Yes, He has. He gave you His own faith as a gift when you received Jesus as LORD. That's how you got saved. As Ephesians 2:8 says, "For by grace you have been saved through faith, and that not of yourselves; it is the gift of God" *(New King James Version)*.

What you need to do now is develop the measure of faith God has already given you (Romans 12:3)—and you don't do that by praying for Him to give you more. The measure of faith is developed by meditating and acting on God's WORD.

Meditating or feeding on The WORD builds your capacity for faith. Exercising your faith by acting on The WORD strengthens and increases it. Think about how you develop your physical body, and you'll get the picture. You start by eating the right foods and taking in the nutrients that provide your muscles with the capacity to grow. Then you strengthen your muscles with the help of weights or some other kind of resistance.

The weights and resistance bands by themselves don't build your strength, of course. For them to help you, you must do something with them. I know this from experience. I owned barbells for years, and I can tell you that as long as I just left them sitting out in the garage, they didn't help me at all. I wished they

Focus on The WORD, Not the Waves

would have. But for them to help develop my muscles, I had to grab them and start sweating.

The same thing is true spiritually. What strengthens your faith isn't just encountering the tests and trials of life. (If tests and trials by themselves were enough, everyone in the world would be a faith giant. But that's not the case.) To develop your faith, you must do something with it. You must push back against the negative, fear-filled, unbelieving, law-of-sin-and-death-dominated flow of the world by saying and doing what God says.

You don't have to wait until you're facing a major test or trial to do that. You can do it when things in your life are going fine. In fact, that's when you should be doing it!

You wouldn't want to wait until some thug broke in your back door to develop your physical strength, would you? You wouldn't want to wait to work out until some criminal came barging in, jerked you up off the couch, slapped the doughnut out of your hand, and said, "Get out of my house! I'm taking over here."

No, that's not the time to go out to the garage and start hunting for your barbells. By then, it's too late. You should have worked out beforehand. Then when the thief showed up at your house, you would have been ready to deal with him. Since you're not, the best thing to do, in the natural, is to get help from the bodybuilder next door.

Spiritually, if you find yourself behind the curve like that, the best thing to do is find another believer who has already worked out and ask him or her to pray and believe God with you. If, for example, you were to receive a critical diagnosis from the doctor and hadn't yet developed your faith for healing, you should get help from a believer who has. You should follow the instructions in James 5 where it says:

LIVE FEAR FREE

Is any sick among you? let him call for the elders of the church; and let them pray over him, anointing him with oil in the name of The LORD: And the prayer of faith shall save the sick, and The LORD shall raise him up; and if he have committed sins, they shall be forgiven him (verses 14-15).

Don't remain dependent on the faith of others, though. Keep developing your own. Study and meditate on healing scriptures and exercise your faith for healing even when you're feeling good. Rather than waiting until you're experiencing symptoms of sickness, declare The WORD over your body every day.

After you do that for a while, if satan attacks you with sickness, he'll run into a brick wall of faith. You'll know that Jesus already paid for your healing and it belongs to you. Instead of thinking you're the sick trying to get healed, you'll know that you are the healed, and satan is trying to steal your health—and you won't let him do it!

If you're just getting started and you've never learned how to meditate on The WORD, it's very simple. Find scriptures you can apply to various areas of your life, and take time to read and fellowship with God over them. Read what the Bible says about faith, for instance, or about righteousness, healing, protection or provision, and keep going over them. Read about God's Love, goodness and faithfulness.

Spend time rehearsing and rejoicing over scriptures that tell you what God has promised and provided for you in Christ. Receive them as God speaking directly to you. Say out loud, "This is talking about *me*. Jesus died for *me*. He healed *me*. Oh, how He loves me!"

If satan tries to get in his two cents by reminding you of your

Focus on The WORD, Not the Waves

past sins, faults and failures, answer him with The WORD. Say, "You get behind me, satan. Jesus bore my sins in His own body on the tree. So, if you want to talk about my sin, you go talk to Jesus about it, because He took it and gave me His righteousness."

As you keep meditating on The WORD, your capacity for faith will grow. You'll find you're not stumbling anymore at the promises of God. You're not so easily distracted by the contrary winds of circumstances. The problems may still be there staring you in the face, but in the light of The WORD, those problems begin to miniaturize. They don't look nearly as formidable to you as they did before.

You begin to think, *Glory to God, I'm a child of the Almighty! I'm the righteousness of God in Christ Jesus. I am born of Him, and He said in 1 John 5:4 that "whatsoever is born of God overcometh the world: and this is the victory that overcometh the world, even our faith."*

The next thing you know, you're acting on The WORD. Instead of allowing satan to scare you into believing the storms of life are going to destroy you, you're standing at the front of the boat, fully confident that Jesus Himself is backing you. You boldly say to the wind and the waves, "In the Name of Jesus, peace! Be still!"

Why Did You Change?

As faith's reciprocal, fear follows the same progression. Only instead of developing as you meditate and act on God's WORD, fear develops as you meditate on the lies of the devil. Jesus said of the devil that "when he speaketh a lie, he speaketh of his own: for he is a liar, and the father of it" (John 8:44). So, the devil can always be expected to lie to you. But he gets especially intense about it when you step out by faith on God's WORD.

LIVE FEAR FREE

Particularly if what you're believing for looks impossible, satan will tell you in every way he can that The WORD is not going to work for you. If you refuse to listen to him and continue in faith calling "things which be not as though they were" (Romans 4:17), he'll say, "You can't do that!"

I remember one of the first times I caught him telling me that lie. It was many years ago when I was first getting started in ministry. Having just begun to travel, I desperately needed a new car. The one I'd been driving was leaking at every joint. So, Gloria and I had determined how much money it would take to buy the automobile we needed and asked God for it.

We released our faith in accordance with what Jesus said in Matthew 18:19: "If two of you shall agree on earth as touching any thing that they shall ask, it shall be done for them of my Father which is in heaven." And because the situation was urgent, we agreed for the money to come in by a certain date.

The date we agreed on was October 30.

When that day came and went without the money coming in, I was sorely disappointed. Still relatively new to the faith life, I felt like saying something negative about it. The disciples said something negative to Jesus that stormy night in the boat in Mark 4:37-38: "God, don't You care that we're going die?"

Before I said anything though, I realized it would be tantamount to saying that Jesus missed it in Matthew 18:19. That couldn't be right! *I* might have missed it. I might have made some mistakes in this situation (and I saw later that I did). But I knew Jesus didn't miss it. His WORD is always true.

As I was thinking about it, The LORD spoke up inside me. *Is My WORD any different today than it was yesterday?*

54

Focus on The WORD, Not the Waves

"No, Sir," I said.

Then, why did you change? He asked.

"Because the 30th was yesterday." I replied.

What does that matter? He said.

Suddenly, I understood what The LORD was trying to get across to me. I caught a glimpse of how limitless He is. So, I picked up my faith again and said, "Hallelujah! I believe I receive that money and that I have it by the 30th!"

I didn't care that according to the calendar the date was the 31st. I kept saying all day long, "Yes, praise God, I have my money by the 30th. My wife and I agreed in faith!"

Finally, satan couldn't stand it anymore.

"You can't do that!" he said.

"I just did!" I told him.

"But the 30th was yesterday."

"So what? I have it by the 30th!"

He didn't know how to respond to that, so he shut up.

I was in another state preaching that week. The day after the service, I found out I'd received an urgent phone call. The caller left his number, so I called him back. "Brother Copeland," he said, "please forgive me. I feel so bad about this. God spoke to me two weeks ago about giving you a certain amount of money, and I didn't do it. Last night, He got all over me for neglecting to send it to you."

"Praise God! I don't doubt it, Brother," I said. "Ship the money on over here. I know just what to do with it."

LIVE FEAR FREE

That was my car money. It was there all the time, but it might not have gotten to me if I had listened to the lies of satan. If I'd let him deceive me into letting go of my faith, there wouldn't have been anything in operation to make sure the man followed through on what The LORD had told him to do.

Don't ever listen to the lies of satan! It will always cost you. His lies are designed to put fear into you, and when fear gets in, faith falters.

The Apostle Peter found this out when he stepped out onto the Sea of Galilee. You've probably read about that situation. Peter was with the other disciples endeavoring to cross the Galilee on yet another windy night, when he saw Jesus (who had stayed behind on the shore to pray) walking toward them on the water. Peter asked Jesus to bid him to come. Jesus said, "Come," and Peter did! He got out of the ship and walked on the water toward Jesus.

> But when he saw the wind boisterous, he was afraid; and beginning to sink, he cried, saying, LORD, save me. And immediately Jesus stretched forth his hand, and caught him, and said unto him, O thou of little faith, wherefore didst thou doubt? (Matthew 14:30–31).

Talk about falling for a lie of the devil! Peter was already walking on the water, yet when satan told him, "You can't do this. The wind is too strong. You'll drown!" Peter believed him.

That doesn't even make good sense. What did the wind have to do with anything? Is it easier to walk on water when the wind is calm? No. Wind or no wind, walking on water is impossible in the natural. So clearly, Peter wasn't being upheld by natural forces. What was keeping him on top of the water was Jesus' word, "Come." Peter was walking by faith on the supernatural power of God's WORD.

Focus on The WORD, Not the Waves

When he got his attention off The WORD and onto the circumstances, however, his faith faltered. He succumbed to fear and saw himself drowning. Peter wasn't drowning! When he cried out to Jesus to save him, he was just *"beginning* to sink." The water probably wasn't even up to his ankles, yet Peter was already talking like he was about to die…all because of a lie.

Of course we, as believers, can't be too hard on Peter. We've all made the same mistake at one time or another. If you think about it, you can probably remember what it was like. One moment you were cruising through life by faith, enjoying being saved, and the next moment you were staring fear in the face. Maybe symptoms of sickness hit your body, or the economy went into a recession, or whatever, and the devil started talking to you.

"You're probably coming down with that deadly disease you heard about on the news that's killing so many people," he might have said. Or, "This economic downturn is going to cost you your job. You'd better not buy that new car; you'll be the first employee your company lays off…blah…blah…blah."

Rather than grabbing your Bible, you started listening to and meditating on those lies. You began worrying. Then maybe your spouse joined in, and you both got into agreement with those lies.

All the while, though, the Spirit of God was speaking to you in a still, small voice. He was bringing The WORD to your remembrance and telling you, *There's no disease anywhere that can stand against My healing power. I'll keep you well. There's no recession that can stop Me from providing for you. No matter what the economy does, I'll supply all your need according to My riches in glory by Christ Jesus.*

LIVE FEAR FREE

What happens when the devil is saying one thing about you and God is saying another?

It all depends on you.

As you're about to see in the next chapter...you are the deciding witness.

CHAPTER 4

YOUR WILL, YOUR CHOICE, YOUR WORDS

CHAPTER 4

Your Will, Your Choice, Your Words

…In the mouth of two or three witnesses
shall every word be established.
(2 Corinthians 13:1)

THERE'S AN EXPRESSION THAT'S WORKED its way into people's conversations recently. You've probably heard it. Someone will flippantly spout off about something, make a pronouncement they probably shouldn't have, and then add with a shrug…"I'm just saying."

Just saying.

As harmless as that expression may sound, it's extremely deceptive. It implies that what we say doesn't make any difference—that our words only reflect what we *think* about reality, they don't actually affect it.

Nothing, however, could be further from the truth. Words are behind everything that happens on this planet. They're what brought it into existence. God *spoke* it into being. He *said*…and there it was.

LIVE FEAR FREE

As believers, we know this very well: The universe didn't just accidentally come together through a random cosmic explosion. No, as Hebrews 11:3 says, "Through faith we understand that the worlds were framed by The WORD of God, so that things which are seen were not made of things which do appear." The first chapter of Genesis lays out the process in more detail.

In the beginning God created the heaven and the earth. And the earth was without form, and void; and darkness was upon the face of the deep. And the Spirit of God moved upon the face of the waters. *And God said, Let there be light: and there was light.* [Or, as it's literally translated from the Hebrew, *God said, Light be! And light was]* (verses 1-3).

There's a reason those are the first verses in the Bible. They set the stage for everything that follows. They also set the stage for how we, as His children, are to live our lives. They tell us not only that He is the Creator but also His method of creation, a method which He considers so vital for us to understand that in Genesis 1 it's repeated time and again:

- *"God said,* Let there be a firmament in the midst of the waters.... *and it was so"* (verses 6-7).

- *"God said,* Let the waters under the heaven be gathered together...*and it was so"* (verse 9).

- *"God said,* Let the earth bring forth grass...*and it was so"* (verse 11).

- *"God said,* Let there be lights in the firmament of the heaven...*and it was so"* (verses 14-15).

- *"God said,* Let the waters bring forth abundantly...and fowl that may fly above the earth..."* (verse 20).

- *"God said,* Let the earth bring forth the living creature... *and it was so"* (verse 24).

Your Will, Your Choice, Your Words

The Bible could have conveyed the information in those verses much more concisely. It could have told us just once that "God said," and then listed everything He called into being. But it doesn't. It tells us over and over that "God said" because this isn't just information. It's a revelation God does not want us to miss. As His earthly sons and daughters, we are to operate like He does, so He wants us to understand this all-important truth:

God creates and gives life with His words.

This planet was dead before God said those things in Genesis 1. It was formless, empty and dark. That's not how He originally created it. According to Isaiah 45:18, He did not create the earth "to be a worthless waste. He formed it to be inhabited" *(Amplified Bible, Classic Edition)*. But the fall of satan in ages past killed it. His rebellion against God brought on the earth a massive destruction that left this planet and the atmosphere around it totally dead.[1]

Yet God was able to bring it back to life…with His words.

God doesn't do anything without saying it. He always creates and changes things by speaking words because that's where the power is. That's where the life is.

In Genesis 1:26, we see that even Adam was created with words. He was spoken into existence when God [or *Elohim* in Hebrew, which refers to the Father, Son and Holy Spirit] said, "Let us make man in our image, after our likeness." The LORD wasn't just thinking out loud there. He wasn't just saying to

---

1 Some Bible scholars believe the pre-Adamic destruction of the earth was caused by a monstrous flood that not only engulfed the entire planet but also filled up the space around it. This is the reason, to make the earth habitable again, in Genesis 1:7, God had to "divide the waters which were under the firmament from the waters which were above." It's also the reason for the water marks on the moon. They were left by the first great deluge that flooded the earth and its atmosphere after satan's fall. In Noah's day, the waters God had divided and set above the earth's atmosphere were released onto the earth. The Flood of Noah wasn't caused just by rain or a sizable thunderstorm. As Genesis 7:11 says, "The fountains of the great deep [were] broken up, and the windows of heaven were opened." As devastating as Noah's Flood was, though, it didn't completely demolish the planet. The previous flood did.

LIVE FEAR FREE

Himself, "Here's an idea: Why don't we make a man?" He was releasing His power. Just as He brought forth light by saying, "Let there be light," He was bringing forth Adam by saying "Let us make man...."

"But Brother Copeland," someone might say, "I thought God made Adam out of the dirt."

No, only his body was formed from the dust of the ground. Adam himself was created when God "breathed into his nostrils the breath, or spirit, of life, and man became a living being" (Genesis 2:7, *Amplified Bible, Classic Edition)*.

Jesus said, "The words that I speak unto you, *they* are spirit, and *they* are life" (John 6:63). God breathed spirit and life into Adam with His words.

One day, years ago, while I was studying this, The LORD showed me how it happened. In a vision, I saw Him holding up Adam's grayish, lifeless body. He had it by the shoulders, and as it hung there in front of Him, I could see it was the same size as God Himself.

God isn't 100 feet tall. Jesus said, "Anyone who has seen Me has seen the Father," and Jesus stands around six feet tall. We can picture what Adam looked like by picturing Jesus. Adam was His exact replica. They looked like twins because they were. Both looked just exactly like their Father. So, when God held up Adam's body, they were eye to eye, nose to nose, and mouth to mouth.

Imagine standing right in front of someone your own size and talking to them. Particularly if you were very close together, where would your words and breath hit them? In the face. Not on the forehead or the throat, but right in the nostrils.

In my vision, that's what I saw happen when God breathed

64

Your Will, Your Choice, Your Words

life into Adam. He spoke into the face of Adam's perfectly formed body and said, "Let us make man in our image, after our likeness: and let them have dominion over the fish of the sea, and over the fowl of the air, and over the cattle, and over all the earth, and over every creeping thing that creepeth upon the earth" (Genesis 1:26). With those words, the breath and Spirit of God flowed into Adam's flesh; flooded it with the glory, power and life force of God Himself; and Adam came alive.

> So God created man in his own image, in the image of God created he him; male and female created he them. And God BLESSED them, and God said unto them, Be fruitful, and multiply, and replenish the earth, and subdue it: and have dominion over the fish of the sea, and over the fowl of the air, and over every living thing that moveth upon the earth (verses 27–28).

The Jewish sages note that of all the creatures on earth, only man was made "a speaking spirit"[2] like God. Only man was given the gift of speech. What did God intend for him to do with this royal gift? The first words Adam heard God say made it clear: He was to be fruitful, multiply, replenish and exercise dominion over the earth.

Just like God, who had BLESSED him, Adam was to operate in THE BLESSING, releasing God's life and power to create and change things by speaking faith-filled words.

---

2 *The Chumash, Artscroll Series,* Mesorah Heritage Foundation, Bereishis/Genesis, Rabbi Nosson Sherman (Brooklyn: Messorah Publications, Ltd.) p. 11.

"OPEN TO ME THE GATES OF RIGHTEOUSNESS"

Can you see now why your words matter so much?

Not only are you living in a world that was created and ordered by words; you came from the same place Adam did. He came out of God, and so did you! When you received Jesus as your LORD, you were "born again, not of corruptible seed, but of incorruptible, by The WORD of God, which liveth and abideth for ever" (1 Peter 1:23). God breathed His own eternal life, glory, power and faith into you and re-created you in the image of Jesus.

Jesus is called "the last Adam" (1 Corinthians 15:45). Through Him, you've been empowered to reign in life by speaking faith-filled words, just as the first Adam did before the Fall. You've been authorized to speak God's WORD by faith and expect it to come to pass for you, just as the Gospels reveal that it did for Jesus.

Once you get hold of this, you'll never be the same! When you realize where you came from and what your words of faith can do, it will absolutely make a tiger out of you. It certainly did me!

People who hear me preach now might think that I was always a faith man, but I wasn't. There was a time in my life when fear crawled up and down my spine and successfully robbed me of the BLESSINGS of God. There was a time when I just accepted the lies the devil told me.

"You're nothing but a lousy, no-good worm," he'd say. "You'll never amount to anything. You'd better not set your goals too high. You're sure to fall short of them. You'll end up being a failure and looking like a fool."

Your Will, Your Choice, Your Words

If I had kept listening to the devil and saying what he says, I would have spent my whole life in anxiety, speaking fear-filled words and watching them come to pass. I never would have experienced the peace that passes understanding that causes others to look at me and think, *That poor dummy hasn't got sense enough to worry.* I never would have known the joy of just relaxing and rolling the care of things over onto my heavenly Father.

But, praise God, I have experienced that joy. I have experienced that peace. Because I found out what The WORD says about me, I no longer have to live in fear of failure, thinking and talking like I'm an unworthy worm. Instead, I can boldly say about myself what Psalm 118 says: "The LORD is on my side; I will not fear…. Open to me the gates of righteousness: I will go into them, and I will praise The LORD" (verses 6, 19).

Sadly, many Christians would never dream of saying the gates of righteousness are open to them. They've been taught to say things like, "I'm not worthy to go through those gates. I'm just an old sinner saved by grace." They think they're just being humble. They have no idea that by taking that attitude, they're agreeing with the devil. But they are.

They're flatly contradicting God's WORD!

His WORD says in Colossians 3:10 that when we were born again, the old sinner we used to be died, and we "put on the new man, which is renewed in knowledge after the image of him that created him." Second Corinthians 5 says that in Christ we are new creatures and have been "made the righteousness of God in him" (verses 17, 21).

As believers, we're to think in line with the New Testament. We're to say what it says about us instead of repeating man-made religious traditions.

LIVE FEAR FREE

We are to practice following the example of the Apostle Paul. He not only penned those verses I just cited from Colossians and 2 Corinthians; he personally saw himself in the light of them. Before he was saved, he persecuted Christians and put them in jail. Before he was saved, he participated in the stoning of Stephen by holding the men's coats while Stephen was being killed. But after Paul was born again, he said this about himself:

We have wronged no man, we have corrupted no man, we have defrauded no man (2 Corinthians 7:2).

I remember the moment the seeming irony of that statement first dawned on me. I jumped up from the desk where I'd been reading my Bible and said, "I caught that man telling a lie! I know from his own testimony that he harmed and defrauded men."

Immediately, the Spirit of The LORD spoke up on the inside of me. His tone of voice was so stern and loud, it froze me right where I stood.

You watch who you call a liar! He said. *The man you're talking about died on the road to Damascus!*

The moment He said it, I realized it was true. In Christ Jesus, the Apostle Paul had become a new man—a new creature in Christ (2 Corinthians 5:17). What's more, he knew it. He believed it. He had meditated on it until he thought and spoke like a man who had gone through the gates of righteousness.

That's what all of us, as believers, are to do. We're to think and talk about ourselves the way God does. We're to keep looking in the Bible at all the doors Jesus has opened for us and saying by faith, "That's my door, and I'm going through it."

Jesus said, "I am the way.... I am the door" (John 14:6; 10:7, *Amplified Bible, Classic Edition*).

68

Your Will, Your Choice, Your Words

He opened to us the door to righteousness and salvation. He opened to us the door to faith, power, health, redemption, deliverance from sin, demons, sickness, poverty and oppression. He opened the door to a fear-free life, so we can step through it and shout:

Glory be to God, I've been washed in the blood of the Lamb! I've been made the righteousness of Almighty God! Sin shall have no dominion over me, for He that's within me is greater than he that's in the world! Jesus Himself bore my sicknesses and carried my diseases, and by His stripes I am healed. I have whatsoever thing I desire when I pray because I believe I receive it! Whatever I ask the Father in Jesus' Name, He gives it to me, that my joy might be made full! I can come boldly to God's throne of grace, receive His overflowing Covenant mercies and lovingkindness, and find grace to help in every time of need because I'm a believer, not a doubter. Hallelujah! Jesus opened the door, and I've come in!

"Well, I'm not comfortable talking like that, Brother Copeland. I'm concerned some people might think I'm just being arrogant."

Some people probably will. But regardless of what others think, you have the right to make those kinds of bold confessions of faith. In fact, given what Jesus has done for you, you have the responsibility to do so.

You don't necessarily have to do it in front of people who, because they don't know what the Bible says, think you're just boasting about yourself. You don't have to "cast your pearls" of faith before people who can't appreciate their value (Matthew 7:6). But don't let anyone or anything discourage you from speaking The WORD.

LIVE FEAR FREE

It's The WORD that will hold you up when the whole world around you is going under. It's The WORD that's going to stand between you and the perils of these last days, putting you over the finish line in victory.

For it to do so, though, you must not only put it in your mouth—you must keep it there. If you only confess The WORD for a while and then let go of it, satan will steal you blind. He'll deceive you, defeat you, beat you up spiritually and physically, and then leave you wondering what happened.

But when you get over on The WORD of God like Jesus did and say, "It is written!" (Matthew 4:4, 7), satan is absolutely no match for you. When you stand against him, "having your loins girt about with truth, and having on the breastplate of righteousness; and your feet shod with the preparation of the gospel of peace; above all, taking the shield of faith.... the helmet of salvation, and the sword of the Spirit, which is The WORD of God" (Ephesians 6:14-17), satan and all the demons of hell will flee from you.

They have no defense against the power of The WORD. They don't want to mess with it, particularly when it's being spoken by faith through the lips of a believer. They tried that once with Jesus and lost everything they had. He stood on The WORD of God in the belly of hell itself. Through the power and glory of God in that WORD, He "spoiled principalities and powers" and "made a show of them openly, triumphing over them in it" (Colossians 2:15).

Jesus made such a spectacle of satan and his crowd that they've regretted it ever since. As 1 Corinthians 2:8 says, if they had known what was going to happen, "they would not have crucified The LORD of glory."

Your Will, Your Choice, Your Words

DON'T PAY FOR THE SAME THING TWICE

The reason your declarations of faith in The WORD of God are so supernaturally powerful is because they are backed by the victory won by The LORD Jesus Christ. Through His Crucifixion, Resurrection and Ascension, He overcame the world and all the forces of hell and made us, as believers, more than conquerors. He paid the full price for us to be set free from the curse of sin and every fear-inducing thing that follows in its wake.

As the Holy Spirit said through the prophet Isaiah many hundreds of years before Jesus went to the cross:

> Surely He has borne our griefs (sicknesses, weaknesses, and distresses) and carried our sorrows and pains [of punishment], yet we [ignorantly] considered Him stricken, smitten, and afflicted by God [as if with leprosy]. But He was wounded for our transgressions, He was bruised for our guilt and iniquities; the chastisement [needful to obtain] peace and well-being for us was upon Him, and with the stripes [that wounded] Him we are healed and made whole (Isaiah 53:4-5, *Amplified Bible, Classic Edition).*

Those verses aren't just some man's idea of what Jesus did for us. They are God's description of it. He painted a picture for us through Isaiah's words of what happened spiritually during the Crucifixion. Then, in Isaiah 54:8, He called Himself "The LORD thy Redeemer." He assured us that because of the marvelous redemption Jesus wrought:

> In righteousness shalt thou be established: thou shalt be far from oppression; for thou shalt not fear: and from terror; for it shall not come near thee. Behold, they shall surely gather together, but not by me: whosoever shall gather together against thee shall fall for thy sake (verses 14-15).

LIVE FEAR FREE

Let me ask you again: Who said that?

Your Redeemer!

To whom did He say it?

To you.

You are the redeemed! You have been redeemed from fear. You have been delivered from terror and oppression. Although in these last days they will increasingly gather together, you don't have to put up with them. You don't have to live in bondage to them, because Jesus paid the price for you to be free.

Personally, I am not going to pay for something that's been paid for already. It's not right! I knew that even before I got born again, and when I got duped into doing it one time, it really upset me. I was in the military at the time in an army hospital down in Georgia. Some folks came through selling Cokes and cigarettes, and I thought that was nice, so I bought some. Afterward, I looked at the bottom of the cigarette package. It said: "Provided free by the Red Cross." That made me mad! Someone had already paid for those things, and I got ripped off and paid for them again.

I didn't like that then, and I don't like it now. I especially despise it when it involves something Jesus paid such a high price to give me. He shed His precious blood to set me free from fear. He literally went through hell so that it could be written of me in verse 14: "Thou shalt be far from oppression; for thou shalt not fear."

As the author and developer of our faith, Jesus hates fear because it opens the door to oppression, and oppression is of the devil (Acts 10:38). The devil is the author and developer of fear. He uses it to gain access to people to control them and to bring to pass his wicked will for their lives.

Your Will, Your Choice, Your Words

The devil cannot do anything to you apart from fear any more than God will do anything for you apart from faith!

"But Brother Copeland," you might say, "sometimes I can't seem to help feeling afraid. Something alarming will happen, and I can't seem to stop my heart from racing and my knees from knocking together."

That's OK. You can refuse to fear anyway. The spiritual force of fear is not a feeling or an emotion. It's not the physical response our bodies sometimes have when faced with apparent danger. Although we've come to associate fear with those things, they're not what put the spiritual force of fear into operation.

What releases fear to operate in your life is believing the lies of the devil and confirming them with the words of your mouth— and whether or not you choose to do that is up to you. You, as a born-again believer, are a free-will agent. It doesn't matter how hard your heart may be hammering or how shaky your knees may be, you get to choose what you believe and say.

God can't make that choice for you, and neither can the devil. Time and again, as long as you live on this earth, you will face situations where God's WORD will be saying one thing to you and the devil will be saying the opposite. You will be standing between them. You will have to choose whether you will agree with God's truth or the devil's lie.

According to 2 Corinthians 13:1: "In the mouth of two or three witnesses shall every word be established." The choice is yours.

It's *your* will.

It's *your* mouth.

You are the establishing witness.

You are the one who will determine what happens in your life.

LIVE FEAR FREE

POSITIVE OR NEGATIVE, THE PROCESS IS THE SAME

How can you make sure you make the right choice when you're suddenly faced with an emergency or you're under pressure?

You prepare yourself in advance. You spend time meditating on God's WORD. As we discussed in Chapter 3, you take a scripture that applies to an area of your life that needs to be strengthened, and read it again and again. You fellowship with God over it, say it out loud, and keep feeding it into your spirit until it's built inside you, and no one can take it away from you.

In my own life, I've meditated on The WORD so much that at times I wake up in the night with scriptures coming out of my mouth. I might just be getting out of bed to check on a noise I heard, and by the time I've taken two or three steps, I'll catch myself quoting The WORD. I don't even have to stop and think about it. It just flows out of me.

That doesn't happen because I'm a preacher. It happens because I consistently put The WORD inside me. I feed on it personally the same way I feed it to other people when I minister. When I'm conducting a series of meetings about fear-free living, for instance, I'll have the congregation turn to Psalm 118:6 in every service. I'll have them read again and again, "The LORD is on my side; I will not fear."

Why doesn't it bother me to keep going back to the same verse? For the same reason it doesn't bother me to eat eggs for breakfast one day and eat them again the next. Just because I had eggs once doesn't mean I'm through eating eggs. If I like them, I can eat them every day.

Just as eggs are food for your body, God's WORD is food for your spirit. You can feed on the same scripture every day for

Your Will, Your Choice, Your Words

as long as you choose, and it will nourish your spirit every time. You'll get to where it becomes so much a part of you that in moments of crisis, it will come out of your mouth without you even having to think about it.

Suppose, for example, you spend time feeding on Psalm 23. Then a bill comes in the mail that you can't see how you're going to pay. Instead of saying, "I don't know what I'm going to do!" you'll say, "The LORD is my shepherd; I shall not want!" You'll automatically start talking as if you already have the money and the financial need is met.

Don't try to tell me you can't believe you have something before you can see it, either. You know very well you can. You've done it in a negative sense all too often. We all have. Maybe you were talking to a co-worker at the office when you suddenly got the chills and said, "Oh no, I must have that awful virus that's been going around. I don't know why I always get that stuff." You didn't have to see that virus to believe you had it. You just accepted it and, without giving it a second thought, started saying you were sick.

Positive or negative, the process is exactly the same. We believe, and therefore we speak. That is what human beings do. It is what causes things to come to pass. There is no other process. It is God's system, and the whole world operates on it. The only thing satan can do is to pervert it. So, that's what he does.

He lies to people and deceives them into becoming the establishing witness to his lies. He tricks people into believing and saying what he says to them instead of what God says, all the while telling them their words don't matter, that they're *just saying.*

As a result, the world is full of people who think they are just stumbling through life and the circumstances they encounter are

LIVE FEAR FREE

just happening to them. But, of course, that too is a lie. The truth is in the Bible. It says:

- "Death and life are in the power of the tongue" (Proverbs 18:21).
- "He that keepeth his mouth keepeth his life" (Proverbs 13:3).
- "He who would love life and see good days, let him refrain his tongue from evil, and his lips from speaking deceit" (1 Peter 3:10, *New King James Version).*
- "He who guards his mouth and his tongue keeps himself from troubles" (Proverbs 21:23, *Amplified Bible, Classic Edition).*
- "By thy words thou shalt be justified, and by thy words thou shalt be condemned" (Matthew 12:37).
- "A good man out of the good treasure of his heart bringeth forth that which is good; and an evil man out of the evil treasure of his heart bringeth forth that which is evil: for of the abundance of the heart his mouth speaketh" (Luke 6:45).

CHAPTER 5

APPLYING AND ACTING ON YOUR FAITH

CHAPTER 5

Applying and Acting On Your Faith

And Jesus answering saith unto them, Have faith in God.
For verily I say unto you, That whosoever shall say unto
this mountain, Be thou removed, and be thou cast into the sea;
and shall not doubt in his heart, but shall believe that those things
which he saith shall come to pass; he shall have whatsoever he saith.
(Mark 11:22–23)

ONCE YOU HAVE MADE THE choice to reject the lies of the devil and begin speaking The WORD of God, the first place your words go to work is inside *you*. As you meditate on them and confess them, they develop faith in your heart. If you are facing some mountainous problem and you have been meditating on Mark 9:23 for instance, "All things are possible to him that believeth," you start seeing that mountain differently. You start thinking in your heart, *That thing is not supposed to be in my way! It's contrary to the promises of God. He's given me victory over it.*

Having faith inside you, however, is only the first step. For it to produce results on the outside, you must apply it. You must release your faith by speaking *to* the mountain.

Many Christians just want to ask God to move the mountain.

LIVE FEAR FREE

But that's not what Jesus told us to do. He never said, "Come talk to Me about it, and if you can talk Me into it, I'll move it." He told us to talk to the mountain and *tell* it to be removed.

To be clear, there is nothing wrong with talking to God about a problem. He may have information that you need. But once you know what His WORD says and you have fellowshipped with Him over it, you put your faith into action. You command the mountain to go. Then you begin to praise and thank God that it's gone.

You might not even see a dent in it yet, but that doesn't matter. You know that when you spoke, something happened in the realm of the spirit. You're confident that your heavenly Father, The LORD Jesus, the Holy Spirit and the angels of God heard you. You're confident that they are backing up what you said, and all the demons in hell can't stop your words from coming to pass.

You know you are the establishing witness in your own life. You know you have the Name of Jesus and the righteousness of God invested in you. You know the mantle of authority over your shoulders has been placed there by the King of kings and LORD of lords, your name is written in the Lamb's Book of Life, and you are a child of the Covenant. You believe the things you say come to pass and know you can have whatever you say.

As we've already seen, however, you aren't the only one who knows all this. The devil and his cohorts do too. That is why they continually try to deceive you and get your testimony to cease.

You have the authority to pull down their strongholds. You have the "power to tread on serpents and scorpions, and over all the power of the enemy" (Luke 10:19). If the devil can't get you somehow or another to exchange your words of faith for words of fear, you can trample him in the dust.

Applying and Acting On Your Faith

You did it when you got born again. If satan could ever have kept your words of faith from working, he would have done it then. But he couldn't. He might have tried. He might have told you that you didn't qualify for the promise in John 3:16. He might have said, "You can't receive everlasting life from God, you unworthy worm. Your sin is too great." But once you made the decision to believe on Jesus and said so, the devil himself could not stop you from being reborn.

If that's not proof enough for you of the power of believing and speaking God's WORD, consider this: Words received from God and spoken in faith by His people over thousands of years are what made the new birth available to you. Faith-filled words are what opened the door for Jesus to be born into the earth.

The very day Adam sinned, God began releasing faith-filled words into the earth to overcome what Adam had set in motion. First, He said to satan in the presence of Adam and Eve, "I will put enmity between you and the woman, and between your seed and her Seed; He shall bruise your head, and you shall bruise His heel" (Genesis 3:15, *New King James Version*). Then He began establishing covenants with people by giving them His WORD, which contained covenant promises that would work for anyone who would receive them.

Among those promises were many that spoke in detail about the coming Redeemer who would crush satan's head and set mankind free. Every time someone received what God said and responded in faith, His plan took another step forward. His WORD was released into the earth and once here, nothing could get it out. Nothing could keep God's promise about the coming Messiah from being fulfilled. For, as The LORD said through the prophet Isaiah:

So shall My WORD be that goes forth out of My mouth:

LIVE FEAR FREE

it shall not return to Me void [without producing any effect, useless], but it shall accomplish that which I please and purpose, and it shall prosper in the thing for which I sent it (Isaiah 55:11, *Amplified Bible, Classic Edition*).

Why was it necessary for God to execute His plan of Redemption through the faith-filled words of His people on earth?

Because He couldn't just do anything here that He wanted anymore. He had limited Himself by giving mankind authority over the earth. So, to reverse the curse brought on it by the first Adam, He needed to create another Adam. A sinless Man who could pay the price for all sin and set people free.

God couldn't create this new Adam, however, like He did the first one. Having given authority to mankind, He couldn't form another body from the dust of the earth and speak words of Spirit and life directly into it. So, He did the same thing another way. He spoke Jesus into the earth through His covenants and the words of the prophets.

The process took longer because it required many words of prophecy to complete it. But when everything had been said about Jesus that had to be said, the inevitable happened: *"The WORD was made flesh,* and dwelt among us" (John 1:14).

Once Jesus was here, He walked in the authority Adam was originally given. He laid aside His divine powers and operated not as God, but as Man. He faced the same temptations and tests Adam faced, but where Adam failed those tests, Jesus passed them.

Matthew 4:4 reveals how He did it. It tells us that when the devil tempted Jesus to command stones to be made bread, He said, "It is written, Man shall not live by bread alone, but by every word that proceedeth out of the mouth of God" (Matthew 4:4).

Applying and Acting On Your Faith

That statement reveals why Jesus walked on earth in total victory, and the devil couldn't touch Him. It wasn't because He is the divine Son of God. It was because He lived on The WORD. He believed it, spoke it and acted on it. When we, as believers, live on The WORD, satan can't touch us either.[3]

THE ROAR HELL WILL NEVER FORGET

"But what about when Jesus went to the cross?" someone might say. "If He was untouchable, why was satan able to get his hands on Him there?"

Because when the time came for Jesus to be crucified, He voluntarily put Himself within satan's reach.

What happened on the Cross was a reenactment of what happened in the Garden of Eden. A Man, by an act of His own will, submitted Himself to satan and became subject to the law of sin and death. But unlike the first Adam, Jesus didn't *commit* sin. By faith, He *took* sin into His own spirit, soul and body, in obedience to God.

The first act by Adam in the Garden of Eden was an act of treason. The second act by Jesus was an act of Love and sacrifice. He bore the law of sin and death *for us,* and that law did the same thing to Him it did to Adam. It separated Him from God. It cut Him off from His Life Source. The moment it did, Jesus cried out, "My God, my God, why hast thou forsaken me?" and began to die (Mark 15:34).

He didn't just die physically, either. He died spiritually and descended into the heart of the earth, where all who are separated from God and from their bodies must go to be incarcerated. We know it as a place called hell. There, all satan's demonic hosts

---

3 "We know that whosoever is born of God sinneth not; but he that is begotten of God keepeth himself, and that wicked one toucheth him not" (1 John 5:18).

LIVE FEAR FREE

set about to annihilate and torment Jesus forever. They planned to keep Him in bondage for eternity. They wanted to stop God from ever having any contact with mankind again, thereby making way for satan to reign on this earth without interference.

But of course, that's not what happened. God had laid a trap for satan. Once Jesus had paid the price for sin and divine justice had been satisfied, the trap was sprung. Jesus declared The WORD of God in the depths of hell itself, was born again and "justified in the Spirit" (1 Timothy 3:16). The power and glory of His heavenly Father invaded that place, and God roared from heaven the words recorded in Hebrews 1:

> Thou art my Son, this day have I begotten thee.... And again, I will be to him a Father, and he shall be to me a Son.... let all the angels of God worship him.... Thy throne, O God, is for ever and ever: a sceptre of righteousness is the sceptre of thy kingdom. Thou hast loved righteousness, and hated iniquity; therefore God, even thy God, hath anointed thee with the oil of gladness above thy fellows.... Sit on my right hand, until I make thine enemies thy footstool (verses 5-13).

God spoke those words to Jesus after He had walked this earth as a Man. He said them after Jesus took on Himself our sin and became spiritually dead, just as we were before we got saved. Speaking to Jesus when raising Him from the dead, He called a born-again Man, "God"!

Think what this means about us as believers.

According to the New Testament, in the mind of the Father, we were reborn at the same time Jesus was. We were chosen "in him before the foundation of the world," and "even when we were dead in sins [God]...quickened us together with Christ"

Applying and Acting On Your Faith

(Ephesians 1:4, 2:5). From God's perspective, we were there, in Christ, when He said to Jesus, *Thy throne, O God, is for ever and ever: a sceptre of righteousness is the sceptre of thy kingdom.*

That means when we received Jesus as our LORD, our spirits were made alive with those same glorious statements! By the power of the Holy Spirit, the same words that raised Jesus from the dead were exercised upon us the moment we believed in Him and we were born again. We were begotten by the Father, and He "raised *us* up together, and made *us* sit together in heavenly places in Christ Jesus" (Ephesians 2:6).

As believers, we are joint heirs with the born-again Man whom the Father called "God"! We don't have any more reason to be afraid of the devil and his crowd than Jesus Himself does! For as Hebrews 2:14-15 says:

> Inasmuch…as the children have partaken of flesh and blood, He Himself likewise shared in the same, that through death He might destroy him who had the power of death, that is, the devil, and release those who through fear of death were all their lifetime subject to bondage *(New King James Version).*

The word translated *destroy* in that passage doesn't mean the devil doesn't exist anymore. He still exists, but when it comes to dealing with us, as believers, he has no real power. He has been "render[ed] inoperative" *(Wuest Translation).* Where we're concerned, he has been brought "to nought" and made "of no effect" *(Amplified Bible, Classic Edition).*

LIVE FEAR FREE

YOU ARE THE BENEFICIARY OF THE WILL

I'm going to keep saying this every way I know how to make sure you get it: You don't have anything at all to fear anymore! Every single destructive thing satan brought on mankind has been dealt with through the resurrection of Jesus. Everything that was stolen through the law of sin and death has been restored and made available to you through the knowledge of Jesus Christ and the blood-ratified, Holy Spirit backed promises recorded in the Bible.

Stop and remember for a moment what the Bible actually is. It's not just a book. It's the written record of God's Covenants.[4] In our day, because people don't use the word *covenant* much anymore, those Covenants are referred to as the Old Testament and the New Testament. The word *testament* is another word for "a will." As I'm sure you know, a will is a legal document that determines how a person's possessions will be distributed after their death.

When you open your Bible and read the New Testament, you're reading a Will. You're reading Jesus' Last Will and Testament!

It records that Jesus bought back everything the devil stole in the Garden of Eden. That all authority in heaven and on earth has been given to Him. That "all the promises of God in Him *are* Yes, and in Him Amen" (2 Corinthians 1:20, *New King James Version),* and that those promises cover everything that pertains to life and godliness. His Will also records that in His death He bequeathed all those things to those named as His beneficiaries and that, in His Resurrection, He has become the Executor of His own Will.

Jesus is the only Man who ever wrote a Will, died, then was

---

4 For a more in-depth study of God's covenants, see the book I wrote with Professor Greg Stephens, *God, The Covenant, and the Contradiction.*

86

Applying and Acting On Your Faith

raised from the dead to see to it His Will was carried out. We as believers, are the beneficiaries of that Will, and its benefits belong to us right now.

As we've already established, we don't have to wait until we die and go to heaven to enjoy those benefits. Though that's sometimes been taught in certain theological circles, it doesn't make sense. If I write a will and make you the beneficiary, the will goes into effect when I die, not when you die.

In heaven, we won't even need many of the benefits Jesus provided for us in His Will. We won't need healing because there's no sickness in heaven. We won't need victory over the devil and his works because the devil won't be there.

We need what's in the Will now, while we're on the earth! Jesus didn't intend for us to live like paupers here. He left us the inheritance of a King, and we have the right to draw on that inheritance every day of our lives. We have a right to lay claim by faith to what's ours and, when the devil tries to lie us out of it, to say to him like Jesus did: "IT IS WRITTEN!"

The choice is ours, though. So, the reciprocal is true as well. We also have the right to just take whatever fearful thoughts the devil brings to our mind and let him walk all over us.

"But Brother Copeland, I'd rather not have to deal with the devil at all. Can't I just tell him once and for all to leave me alone so I won't be bothered with fearful thoughts anymore?"

No, that's not an option. Although the devil is a defeated foe, he still has the right to bring thoughts to you, and he's going to do it. As 1 Peter 5:8 says, he still "walketh about, seeking whom he may devour." So, if you don't want to be devoured, your only option is to guard your mind and refuse to take any thoughts that don't line up with God's WORD.

LIVE FEAR FREE

Jesus taught us to do this in Matthew 6. After commanding us not to worry about money and material provision, He said:

Take no thought, saying, What shall we eat? or, What shall we drink? or, Wherewithal shall we be clothed? (For after all these things do the Gentiles seek:) for your heavenly Father knoweth that ye have need of all these things. But seek ye first the kingdom of God, and his righteousness; and all these things shall be added unto you (verses 31-33).

Notice, Jesus didn't tell us to *have* no thoughts. That would be impossible. As long as we have a functioning brain, we're going to have thoughts. What Jesus said was, *"Take* no thought, *saying...."* It's what we say that determines whether we take a thought or reject it.

Have you ever noticed that the moment you start to speak, your head has to shut up and listen to what your mouth has to say? Try it and you'll see it's true. Start counting silently from one to ten and while you're counting, say your name out loud. What happened to your counting when you said your name? It stopped.

This is the secret to "casting down imaginations, and every high thing that exalteth itself against the knowledge of God, and bringing into captivity every thought to the obedience of Christ" (2 Corinthians 10:5). You cast down thoughts with the words of your mouth!

If some kind of worldwide pandemic hits and satan brings you the thought that it might harm you, you cast that thought down by saying the opposite. You immediately start speaking The WORD of God. You start declaring what it says about your healing.

You quote Psalm 91:3 for instance. You say, "Surely my God shall deliver me from the snare of the fowler and from the perilous

Applying and Acting On Your Faith

pestilence." You don't just say it once, either. You say it every time that pandemic comes to mind.

Why must you keep on saying it? Because at first, you'll just be saying that verse as a thought. But as you keep taking it by saying it, that verse will get down into your spirit.

Proverbs 20:27 says, "The spirit of man is the candle of The LORD, searching all the inward parts of the belly." When a thought from God's WORD gets transferred from your mind into your spirit, it goes from being just a thought to being a revelation. It starts coming out of your mouth without you having to take the thought and say it, because it's coming not from your head but from your spirit.

Words that come from your spirit produce greater results! They work mightily because they are filled with the Anointing and the life force of God that's within you.

As a born-again spirit being, you can have the life force of God surging inside of you so powerfully that it not only affects you, but also flows out of you to influence those around you. You can have enough of God's healing power flowing out of your spirit that it keeps your own body well, and when others are sick you can lay hands on them, and they can be healed.

DON'T MAKE A POOR TRADE

How many times must you take a thought from The WORD of God and say it before it gets down in your spirit? I can't tell you. All I can tell you is that if you stick with the process, it will happen—and when it does, your words will release God's mountain-moving power.

I've seen that process work time and again. I remember one time in the early years of my ministry, for instance, I had traveled

LIVE FEAR FREE

to Omaha, Nebraska, to preach some meetings in the Fontenelle Hotel. The night before the meetings were to begin, as I was lying in bed in the hotel, all the symptoms of the flu came on me. Within three minutes, I was sick as a horse. (That's sick, BIG.) I hurt from the top of my head to the bottom of my feet.

Immediately, the devil hit me with thoughts of fear. "You're scheduled to preach three services a day for the next three days, and you're going to be too sick to do it," he said. "You've already preached here before and told these people about all this faith stuff, and you're going to die before the meetings start tomorrow!"

At that moment, I felt like taking those thoughts and agreeing with them. I didn't feel like declaring The WORD of God and standing in faith. I didn't want to rebuke those flu symptoms. I didn't want to do any of it! I didn't even want to preach. I wanted to go home, get in my own bed, and let someone rub my fevered brow. But instead, I grabbed my Bible and read some healing scriptures.

By the time I swung my legs out of the bed, I was confessing The WORD. I was saying, "By His stripes I am healed! Himself bore my sicknesses and carried my diseases! I refuse to fear the flu! I refuse to be sick! I won't lay down under these lying symptoms! I will preach these meetings, come hell or high water! I will preach and not stop, as long as Jesus Christ is on the throne. So, satan, you can do yourself a favor and get out of here, because I'm going to take The WORD of God and rip you apart with it!"

Beside the bed, there was a big, bare spot on the floor and, being winter, that spot was very cold. As I started to put my foot down on it, this thought occurred to me: *Don't put your foot on that cold floor without your house shoes on; the cold will make your nose run.* I had already slipped one foot into my house shoe before the thought came, and I realized as I put on

90

Applying and Acting On Your Faith

the other shoe, I had acted in agreement with it.

Kicking both house shoes off, I said, "I refuse to act on that thought! In the Name of Jesus, I'll go to the meeting barefooted if I must!" Then, I stood right there on that spot and confessed The WORD…for forty-five minutes. I kept count of how many times I did it. I thanked God for my healing, declared the scriptures, and resisted satan 529 times without experiencing anything except a very dry, sore throat.

But the 530th time I declared God's WORD, His power hit me right behind my neck, shot all the way down to my feet, and came shooting back up my neck again. It ran that flu out of my body, and I had a running, jumping-up-and-down, rejoicing fit right there in that hotel room!

I preached the services as planned, and on the first night I invited people to come up and receive the Baptism in the Holy Spirit. As I started laying hands on them, the manifest presence of God hit the place. People started speaking in tongues and falling under the power of God until at last count there were 150 of them laid out on the floor. Some people got healed. Others ran down the aisles toward the platform where I was ministering, and the power of God came on them with such force it knocked them backward.

Wouldn't it have been pitiful to have traded all that for the flu?

Certainly it would! But I would have done it if I had taken the fear-based thoughts satan presented to me. I would have wound up letting him talk me out of what the Bible says. If I had listened to the devil's lies, I would have stopped declaring The WORD before I hit that 530th time, because he was telling me my healing wasn't going to come.

Let me help you get this settled in your mind: *Healing always*

LIVE FEAR FREE

comes! It's not always received, but it always comes because it's already here. It's here because Jesus has already provided it. It's here because on the Day of Pentecost, the Holy Spirit invaded the earth's atmosphere with enough of God's power to save everyone on this planet from spiritual death and get them born again. He healed and delivered them from every work of the devil, a thousand times over.

The Bible says the free gift of righteousness has come "upon *all*" (Romans 5:18), and healing is one of the benefits of righteousness. All aren't receiving it, but it has come. It's here and available to any person anywhere, anytime. It can be received by anyone who will receive it by believing and acting on God's WORD!

THE FORCES OF THE SPIRIT ARE MORE POWERFUL THAN THE FLESH

My actions were what the devil was after when he presented me with the thought in the hotel that day about not stepping on the cold floor. He not only wanted to stop me from speaking The WORD, He wanted to get me to *act* on the fear-filled thoughts he was bringing me.

Taking the devil's thoughts and saying them produces fear; acting on fear produces failure.

It's a deadly progression. You might think that giving in to fear is no big deal, that you can act on it just once and that will be the end of it. But it won't. The first fear-based action you take is just the beginning. "Fear hath torment" (1 John 4:18), and with every fear-driven step you take, the torment gets worse. Given the opportunity, satan will keep pushing you to act on fear until it's so developed in you, it completely twists your thinking.

I've known of people who became so highly developed in fear

Applying and Acting On Your Faith

that when they got sick and needed surgery, the doctor wouldn't operate on them. One friend of mine who got himself in that state called my mother from the hospital in the middle of the night. "Mrs. Copeland, I need you to pray for me," he said. "Somehow fear has clutched me and taken such authority over me that it's killing me."

When she got there to minister to him, she found out he'd been taken to surgery but sent back to his room because the anesthesiologist had refused to administer the anesthetic. "This man has too much fear," the anesthesiologist said. "If he gets out of control of his faculties, he'll die."

My mother laid hands on the man in his hospital room, spoke to the spirit of fear in the Name of Jesus and drove it out. After it was gone, the man didn't have to have surgery because he got well.

This is where we've missed it many times in dealing with sickness. We've focused on its outward manifestations. We've struggled against it in the flesh. But as Ephesians 6:12 says, we don't wrestle "against flesh and blood."

Our fight of faith is against satan and his evil spirits; and they work through fear. When we shut down fear, we shut down their power source and strip them of their ability to keep sickness on us. On the other hand, when we speak and act on God's WORD, His power and the Anointing of His Spirit within us can flow freely and minister healing to our bodies.

The forces and fruit of God's indwelling Spirit are far mightier than anything that might be wrong in our flesh! They're mightier than even the deadliest of diseases. I know it because that's what The WORD says and I know it from experience.

Some years ago when she was eleven years old, my granddaughter Lyndsey contracted the life-threatening disease Neisseria

LIVE FEAR FREE

meningitis. She woke up with it one Christmas morning, so sick she was delirious. They rushed her to Cook Children's Medical Center in Fort Worth, and after looking at her spinal fluid, the specialist said she probably wouldn't live through the night.

Lyndsey's mother, my daughter Kellie, was the first to get the news. She told me later that when she first heard it, fear instantly gripped her. "It came down on me like a black shroud," she said. "It felt heavy and strong." But Kellie knew better than to yield to that fear.

Instead, she did what Jesus told Jairus to do in Luke 8:50. When Jairus got the news that his daughter had died, Jesus said, "Fear not: believe only, and she shall be made whole." So, Kellie, after hearing Lyndsey's dire medical prognosis, chose to *believe only*. Walking over to her sister, Terri, who was there with her in the hospital waiting room, Kellie looked her in the eye and said, "I REFUSE TO FEAR!"

Afterward, she told me about what happened. "Daddy, when I said those words, the fear left. It didn't have any power at all. It just flew away." When it did, she knew she had the victory.

Gloria and I were 650 miles away at the time. They called us about Lyndsey, and we immediately flew to Fort Worth. During the flight, we just prayed in the spirit and listened for The LORD's instructions. By the time we reached Fort Worth, at about 11 that night, I had heard from The LORD what to do when I saw Lyndsey. He said, *Put your index finger on her breastbone and say, Lyndsey, I speak to the anointing on the inside of you. Rise up and put this disease out of this body.*

When we arrived at the hospital, we donned HAZMAT suits as required. Then, with Gloria on one side of Lyndsey's bed and me on the other, I did just exactly as The LORD had directed.

94

Applying and Acting On Your Faith

Lyndsey, who at eleven years old was already born again and baptized in the Holy Spirit, responded with fierce faith. She gritted her teeth and hollered as loud as she could, "Pawpaw, I'm healed in the Name of Jesus!"

The doctors kept her in the hospital eight days after that for observation, then sent her home, free of every trace of that life-threatening meningitis bacteria. Totally healed!

PRACTICE WALKING IN THE FAITH THAT OVERCOMES THE WORLD

You don't have to wonder how you would respond in that kind of situation. You already know. You would do what you've practiced. If, on a daily basis, you've practiced speaking and acting by faith in The WORD of God, that's what you'll do in moments of crisis. If you've practiced speaking and acting on fear in seemingly unimportant matters of life, that's what you'll do when you're faced with something important.

"But I've developed such a habit of speaking fear that I do it without realizing it," someone might say. "I'm not sure I can change that."

You don't have to change it on your own. You can ask God to help you. You can pray, as the psalmist of old did, "Set a guard, O LORD, before my mouth; keep watch at the door of my lips" (Psalm 141:3, *Amplified Bible, Classic Edition*).

Take a moment and pray that right now. Say, "Heavenly Father, reveal to me when I'm speaking fear and don't realize it. Point it out to me so that I can renounce words of fear and replace them with words of faith." Then let The LORD help you get ready to act on what He shows you. When you're meditating on The WORD and fellowshipping with Him, practice seeing

LIVE FEAR FREE

yourself walking through various situations in the faith that overcomes the world.

As a pilot, for many years I've practiced seeing myself deal successfully with all kinds of aviation emergencies. These days, this can be done in sophisticated flight simulators that perfectly replicate the experience of flying an airplane. But back in the days before such equipment existed, my simulator was my living room. Sitting in my armchair with everything quiet, as if I were sitting in the cockpit of an airplane, I envisioned running through the preflight checklist. I mentally located every switch. I saw myself firing up the engines and taxiing down the runway.

Many times, during those armchair simulations, I had a flat tire while I was taxiing out. It's a lot easier to think through what to do in that situation when you're sitting in the living room than it would be sitting on a real-life runway. If I were on a runway the first time a tire on my aircraft blew out, I might get flustered. Especially if I had a 747 sitting right behind me, burning up fuel and unable to get around me, I might tear up my airplane trying to get it out of the way.

When you practice handling those situations in advance, you're ready for them. Because you've had time to figure out and meditate on how to handle them, you respond exactly as you should. So, sitting in my living room, I lost engine after engine. I had double-engine failures on approaches. I faced every aviation crisis I could imagine, over and over, and I saw myself coming through them just fine.

When I began learning to live by The WORD of God, I realized I could do the same when it comes to operating by faith. I realized God's BOOK is my checklist for life. It's the Manufacturer's Handbook!

Applying and Acting On Your Faith

An airplane manufacturer's handbook will tell you how to successfully operate the aircraft. It will tell you, for instance, what makes the heater work. You don't have to wait until you're 15,000 feet in the air where it's 10 below zero and just start punching buttons, trying to figure out how to get heat. You can find out in advance that the heating system has safety precautions built into it and that it will only work one way—the way it says in the book!

That's how it is with the power of God. It has safety precautions built into it. It's designed so that you can access it but satan can't. By reading God's BOOK, you can find out how His power system works. You can study it, fellowship with Him over it, and practice implementing it in every situation.

You can be sitting in your living room just feeling great, in good shape financially, safe as can be, and pick up your Bible and meditate on the scriptures about healing, prosperity and protection. You can rehearse what you would do if symptoms of sickness came on you, or the economy crashed, or you were faced with some life-threatening danger. You can envision yourself taking authority over fear, confessing the Scriptures, and rebuking the lies of the devil.

It's like being in a flight simulator. You're not really facing those situations. The devil didn't bring them to you. You presented them to yourself so you could practice acting on The WORD. You envisioned them not in fear but in faith, and thought them through in the light of the Scriptures, so that you'll be ready to overcome any challenge that comes your way.

When God was getting Joshua ready to lead the Israelites into the Promised Land, He said to him:

> This Book of the Law shall not depart out of your mouth, but you shall meditate on it day and night, that you may

LIVE FEAR FREE

observe and do according to all that is written in it. For then you shall make your way prosperous, and then you shall deal wisely and have good success (Joshua 1:8, *Amplified Bible, Classic Edition*).

That's as true for you as it was for Joshua. So prepare yourself to have good success in these last days by keeping The WORD in your mouth. Meditate on it and observe yourself doing all that is written in it. See yourself receiving healing and putting sickness under your feet. See yourself laying hands on the sick and watching them recover. See yourself living in the protection of the secret place of the Most High and being supplied, even in times of famine, with such abundance that you can give to every good work.

You can do that to the point where satan doesn't know what to do with you. He can't throw something at you that catches you off guard because you've already prepared for it. You've been there in your times of meditation, and you already have the victory!

CHAPTER 6

WHEN YOU STAND PRAYING

CHAPTER 6

WHEN YOU
STAND PRAYING

*Therefore I say unto you, What things soever ye desire,
when ye pray, believe that ye receive them, and ye
shall have them. And when ye stand praying, forgive,
if ye have ought against any: that your Father also
which is in heaven may forgive you your trespasses.
(Mark 11:24–25)*

A FEAR-FREE LIFE IS A life of answered prayer. It's a life where you don't have to be afraid of anything, because God has promised and provided us with everything. It's a life where we operate according to the Manufacturer's Handbook, confident that just as Jesus said, we can believe and receive from God whatever we ask.

Notice, Jesus did not say we *might* get what we ask. Nor did He say we would receive what we asked *every once in a while*. No, He said something that sounds almost too good to be true. He said when we ask God for something believing we receive, we *shall* have it.

In other words, when we pray in faith, we can get what we ask for every time.

Sadly, such a level of victory in prayer seems unattainable to

LIVE FEAR FREE

many believers. Even though they know Jesus promised it, they don't really expect to experience it on a day-to-day basis. Instead, thinking they don't qualify for it right now, they put it off into the future. While they do hope to receive answers to some of their prayers while they're still living in this flawed and fallen world, they figure that to actually receive "what things soever" they desire when they pray, they'll have to wait until they get to heaven where everything is perfect.

Jesus, however, wasn't talking about heaven in Mark 11:24-25! He was answering the questions His disciples had asked about the fig tree. If you've read the passage, you'll remember what happened.

The previous day, Jesus had spoken to that tree after finding leaves on it but no fruit. "No man eat fruit of thee hereafter for ever," He'd said (verse 14). Less than twenty-four hours later, the tree had withered away. When His disciples saw it and expressed their amazement, Jesus taught them how to speak and pray in faith, and get the same kind of results.

That was an earthly fig tree, not a heavenly one! It was used by Jesus as an example of what happens when we access and release God's power to change things here on earth. With that in mind, read again what He said:

> Have faith in God. For verily I say unto you, That whoso-
> ever shall say unto this mountain, Be thou removed, and
> be thou cast into the sea; and shall not doubt in his heart,
> but shall believe that those things which he saith shall
> come to pass; he shall have whatsoever he saith. Therefore
> I say unto you, What things soever ye desire, when ye pray,
> believe that ye receive them, and ye shall have them. And
> when ye stand praying, forgive, if ye have ought against
> any: that your Father also which is in heaven may forgive
> you your trespasses (verses 22–25).

When You Stand Praying

Not only does Jesus make it clear in this passage that these principles of faith and prayer are for us here and now, He also tells us they'll work for "whosoever" chooses to apply them. They're not just for apostles or prophets or specially called ministers. Anyone who will do what Jesus said there can ride the tide of God's power to victory just as He did when He was on earth.

It's time we stopped thinking such victory is beyond our reach!

If it was beyond our reach, it would have been unjust for Jesus to promise it. If there's no way for us to walk in that level of victory, it would be a miscarriage of justice for God to say in 1 John 5:4 that "this is the victory that overcometh the world, even our faith." God is not unjust, and neither is Jesus. So, the victorious life of overcoming faith and answered prayer must be attainable.

The life of faith is not a life where there ceases to be any more problems. It's not a utopia where there are no mountains and no unfulfilled desires or reason to pray. A fear-free, victorious life is one where we receive from God solutions to seemingly unsolvable problems and, by faith in His WORD, command the mountains the devil has erected in our lives to get out of our way.

"But Brother Copeland," someone might say, "I've done what Jesus said to do in Mark 11:22-24 and it hasn't worked for me. What could be the problem?"

Most likely, you'll find it in verse 25 where Jesus said, "When ye stand praying, forgive, if ye have ought against any." That verse is just as important as the two that precede it. It's a continuation of Jesus' teaching on faith.

Faith and forgiveness are connected.

Faith won't work in an unforgiving heart because "faith… worketh by Love" (Galatians 5:6), and Love forgives. How do

LIVE FEAR FREE

we know Love forgives? Because God is Love, and He forgives us (1 John 1:9; Ephesians 4:32).

Forgiveness is one of faith's built-in safety precautions. Faith will only function properly when it's in place. If you think about it, the reason is obvious. Imagine what you might inadvertently do with faith's mountain-moving power if it worked for you even when you were operating in strife and unforgiveness. You might get mad at some fellow who cut in front of you on the freeway, yell, "Get off the road, you dummy!" and send the poor guy sailing off into the ditch.

Thank God, faith isn't designed to work that way. You can't accidentally use it to harm someone If you ignore its safety precautions, however, you will wind up getting in trouble yourself.

Why?

Because there are only two spiritual kingdoms operating in the earth: God's and satan's, and if you're not operating in one, you're operating in the other.

The only way to walk in victory is by operating in the kingdom of God, and His is a kingdom of faith and Love. Satan's is a kingdom of fear, selfishness and strife, and when you step over into his territory, you step over into defeat. Unforgiveness puts you into satan's territory. It opens the door for him to treat you like his subject. A form of strife, it will always mess up your life because as James 3:16 says, "where envying and strife is, there is confusion and every evil work."

When I first began learning to live by faith, I didn't fully understand this. So, I was confused when I saw satan getting in and tearing up things in my life even after I had prayed and released my faith over them. I knew the problem wasn't with God. He is always right, and He is far bigger than the devil. Therefore, the

When You Stand Praying

problem had to be on my end. Realizing I must be missing it some way or another, I began seeking The LORD to find out how.

As I prayed about it, I remembered that Acts 1:8 says when we're baptized in the Holy Spirit, we receive power—the *dunamis,* energizing, enabling, supernatural, explosive power of God. "LORD," I said, "that power is not functioning in my life as it should. When I run into certain problems, it seems like I get up over them by faith and then they push me right back down."

I told Him I'd seen the same thing happen to other believers. I'd seen them pray and go into business, for instance, believing to prosper. But then the devil would get involved somehow and destroy them financially. "LORD, I want to know what the problem is here," I said.

I was familiar with the statement Jesus made in Mark 11 about forgiving. Back then though, I hadn't yet fully grasped the importance of it. So, The LORD directed me to Matthew 18 where Jesus taught about the prayer of agreement and dealing with discord in the Church. He especially drew my attention to the last part of the chapter.

In verses 21-22, *Amplified Bible, Classic Edition,* Peter asked Jesus, "LORD, how many times may my brother sin against me and I forgive him and let it go? [As many as] up to seven times?"

Jesus replied, "I tell you, not up to seven times, but seventy times seven!"

Therefore the kingdom of heaven is like a human king who wished to settle accounts with his attendants. When he began the accounting, one was brought to him who owed him 10,000 talents [probably about $10,000,000], and because he could not pay, his master ordered him to be sold, with his wife and his children and everything that

LIVE FEAR FREE

he possessed, and payment to be made. So the attendant fell on his knees, begging him, Have patience with me and I will pay you everything. And his master's heart was moved with compassion, and he released him and forgave him [cancelling] the debt. But that same attendant, as he went out, found one of his fellow attendants who owed him a hundred denarii [about twenty dollars]; and he caught him by the throat and said, Pay what you owe! So his fellow attendant fell down and begged him earnestly, Give me time, and I will pay you all! But he was unwilling, and he went out and had him put in prison till he should pay the debt. When his fellow attendants saw what had happened, they were greatly distressed, and they went and told everything that had taken place to their master. Then his master called him and said to him, You contemptible and wicked attendant! I forgave and cancelled all that [great] debt of yours because you begged me to. And should you not have had pity and mercy on your fellow attendant, as I had pity and mercy on you? And in wrath his master turned him over to the torturers (the jailers), till he should pay all that he owed. So also My heavenly Father will deal with every one of you if you do not freely forgive your brother from your heart his offenses (verses 23-35, *Amplified Bible, Classic Edition*).

As I read those verses that day, I was reminded—as you probably were just now—of how freely God has forgiven us. He forgave us of a sin debt that we had no way to pay. He supernaturally eradicated it from His own consciousness and treated us as if we never owed it. He threw the memory of our sin as far from Him as the east is from the west.

As I read about the servant who had been forgiven by his master refusing to do the same for his fellow servant, I was also

When You Stand Praying

reminded that God commands us, as believers, to behave differently. He commands us to be kind to one another, tenderhearted, forgiving one another, even as He forgave us (Ephesians 4:32). I assumed I had done that. As far as I knew, I wasn't carrying around any major grudges or harboring unforgiveness against anyone who had done me wrong. To my knowledge, neither were the other people of faith whom I had seen get ambushed by the devil.

"LORD, I'm not sure I understand what You're trying to get across to me," I said.

Son, He replied, *it wasn't a $10 million debt the servant failed to forgive; it was a $20 debt. Forgiving big trespasses isn't usually where you get tripped up. Most of the time, it's the little 15-cent offenses that are giving My people trouble.*

When I asked Him to help me see exactly what He meant, He instantly gave me a vision. In it, I saw a pipe several feet long and about five inches in diameter. It was tilted over a man's head at a forty-five-degree angle, and water was gushing into the upper end of it. The lower end was about ten inches from the man's face. He was peering into it, looking for the water, but all that was coming out was a fine mist. It was spraying out of a tiny hole in the center of the pipe, hitting the man in the face with just enough water to make him mad.

The pipe is your reborn human spirit, The LORD said. *I am pouring My power into it but not much of it is getting through. I'm not the One holding it back, you are. Over a period of time, you have let little 15-cent and $20 offenses—a little discord here and a little resentment there—get into the pipe. Because you weren't spiritually aware enough to stop it from happening, you've clogged up your spirit until My power does not have the freedom to flow through you. You're too full of unforgiveness and aggravation toward people whom you've never purposely taken the time to forgive.*

How Unforgiveness Stops Us From Living in Victory

Second Corinthians 7:1 says, "Therefore, having these promises, beloved, let us cleanse ourselves from all filthiness of the flesh and spirit" *(New King James Version).* Unforgiveness is spiritual filthiness. It works in a wounded spirit the way dirt does when it gets into a wound in the physical body. It keeps the wound from healing.

Your heart might have been wounded by something hurtful someone said or did; and even though it happened years ago, because you never forgave the person, the wound is still there. You may have learned to live with it. You may even have forgotten about it. But whether you're aware of it or not, until the unforgiveness is removed, that wound will continue to fester and inhibit the flow of God's power in your life.

As I was praying about this after I had the vision, The LORD made a very sobering statement to me. He said, *Unforgiveness and strife stop the things I have put in the Body of Christ to make it victorious.*

What things do strife and unforgiveness stop?

First, they stop us from receiving revelation knowledge from God and His WORD; and without that we can't live in any degree of victory at all. Revelation knowledge is literally the foundation upon which we, as believers and the Church, are built.

Jesus Himself said so! In Matthew 16, He said to Peter who had just announced his great revelation about Jesus being the Christ, the Son of the living God, "Flesh and blood hath not revealed it unto thee, but my Father which is in heaven.... and upon this rock"— of revelation knowledge from God—"I will build my church; and the gates of hell shall not prevail against it" (verses 17-18).

When You Stand Praying

Jesus also referred to revelation knowledge of The WORD as our foundation in Luke 6 where He said, "Whosoever cometh to me, and heareth my sayings, and doeth them, I will show you to whom he is like: He is like a man which built an house, and digged deep, and laid the foundation on a rock: and when the flood arose, the stream beat vehemently upon that house, and could not shake it: for it was founded upon a rock" (verses 47-48).

Without revelation knowledge from God's WORD, we won't have anything solid upon which to build our lives. We won't have what we need to mature spiritually and grow strong in The LORD. So our growth will remain stunted, and we'll get stuck in spiritual infancy.

That's what happened with the believers in the city of Corinth in the Apostle Paul's day. All their fussing with one another turned them into a bunch of spiritual babies. Their ability to receive revelation became so limited that in his letter to them the Apostle Paul wrote:

I, brethren, could not speak to you as to spiritual people but as to carnal, as to babes in Christ. I fed you with milk and not with solid food; for until now you were not able to receive it, and even now you are still not able; for you are still carnal. For…there are envy, strife, and divisions among you… (1 Corinthians 3:1-3, *New King James Version).*

It wasn't that the Corinthian believers weren't interested in growing spiritually. They were! They were especially eager to walk in God's power and operate in the gifts of the Spirit and, to a degree, they were doing it. Yet because of the strife in their midst, the power wasn't accomplishing through them what God intended. So in his letter, Paul told them to stop the strife and walk in Love.

LIVE FEAR FREE

For "though I speak with the tongues of men and of angels, but have not Love," he wrote, "I have become sounding brass or a clanging cymbal. And though I have the gift of prophecy, and understand all mysteries and all knowledge, and though I have all faith, so that I could remove mountains, but have not Love, I am nothing" (1 Corinthians 13:1–2, *New King James Version*).

The day I had the vision of the clogged pipe, The LORD took me through these scriptures and others to show me how strife and unforgiveness cost us spiritually. As I read them and applied them to my own life, I thought, *It's a wonder The LORD has been able to get any power through my spiritual pipe at all!*

Determined to make a change, I took immediate action. I prayed right then and there and purged all the unforgiveness out of me.

When I did, I realized I had gotten hold of something very strong. So, when Gloria walked in the door a few minutes later, I shared it with her. We committed from that time forward to never allow strife or unforgiveness to operate in our marriage or our home.

We've been married more than sixty years now, and we've never had an argument. In years past, I would occasionally shoot my mouth off at her about something, but she never snapped at me in return. She just stayed in Love. I would always apologize to her later, but eventually I learned to stay in harmony with her just as she does with me. As a result, we've seen fulfilled in our lives the promise Jesus made in Matthew 18:19: "If two of you agree on earth concerning anything that they ask, it will be done for them by My Father in heaven" *(New King James Version)*.

After I shared with Gloria that day what The LORD had shown me about purging our hearts of unforgiveness, I shared the

When You Stand Praying

same revelation at the meeting where I was scheduled to preach that night, and the power of God manifested mightily. I couldn't recall ever having experienced His power to that degree in one of my meetings. Everywhere I turned, it was right there.

When I got back to Fort Worth, I preached the same sermon to my staff. "There will be no more strife in this ministry," I said. They took the message to heart, started acting on it and, immediately, the devil came (as he always does) to steal The WORD.

Suddenly, opportunities for us to fuss with each other abounded. It seemed like everyone wanted to fight everyone over the pettiest stuff imaginable. But thank God, bit by bit we got the victory. We kept purging our spiritual pipes by running The WORD of God through them, cleaning them out until there was no strife or unforgiveness left.

Once we, as a staff, were in harmony with each other, we prayed in agreement for the ministry to increase and believed we received. In less than ninety days, this ministry doubled. Everything we were doing doubled!

These days, if I see things start getting fouled up, I check right away for unforgiveness and strife and make sure we're operating in Love. So does my staff. They know how to function together. They know how to pray and believe God together. They know to forgive when they stand praying—and their prayers produce results.

Have we gotten crosswise with each other on occasion? Yes. If the aggravation was on my end, sometimes rather than say anything to them about it, I've gone to God instead and just dealt with it in prayer. Other times, I haven't handled things as well. I've made mistakes just as they have. But God knew we'd mess up sometimes. That's why He told us in 1 John 1:9: "If we confess

111

LIVE FEAR FREE

our sins, he is faithful and just to forgive us our sins, and to cleanse us from all unrighteousness."

FOUR STEPS TO TAKE NOW

First John 1:9 is God's fail-safe system!

It works much like such systems do in the natural. They're designed to go into operation when a primary system doesn't work as intended. For example, in the early 1900s the Hudson automobile introduced a fail-safe braking system. It was engineered so that if, for some reason, the primary, or hydraulic, brake failed to hold, a set of mechanical brakes was activated and prevented potential disaster.

In God's plan for us, His primary will is for us to always walk in Love and faith and to avoid sin so that the wicked one touches us not. (See 1 John 5:18.) But when we fall short of His primary will, His backup plan is for us to stay out of the devil's reach by acting on 1 John 1:9.

Once we confess our sin to God and receive His forgiveness, as far as the devil is concerned, it's as if we never sinned. He can't get his hands on us because God has cleansed us from all unrighteousness and declared us to be as righteous as Jesus.

We don't have to wait until we get to church on Sunday to put God's fail-safe system into operation, either. We don't even have to wait until we can get alone in our prayer closet. Anytime we mess up, we can immediately confess our sin and receive our forgiveness and cleansing.

One time, I had to do that while I was riding in a car with some believers who had been criticizing a particular minister. I hadn't initiated the conversation. But I had joined in with them, talking about how wrong this minister was in what he was doing and

When You Stand Praying

preaching. Suddenly, The LORD spoke to me so loudly I thought everyone in the car heard it. Looking around at them I could see they hadn't, and I was glad because He really scolded me.

What do you think you're doing, talking about your Christian brother that way? He said.

LORD, I'm just listening to and agreeing with everyone else in the car, I replied.

Cut it out! He said. *Don't enter into their conversation anymore. It's putting you into discord with the minister they're discussing, and getting you over into a place where you're subject to torment and the things of the devil.*

Not wanting to spend even a moment more in the devil's territory, I immediately repented and prayed, *LORD, I acknowledge I was wrong. I shouldn't have said those things, and I'm asking You to forgive me. But there's something that's still bothering me.* (When you're talking to God, you might as well be totally honest. He knows what you're thinking anyway.) *The things being said about that minister in this conversation are true!*

How do you know they're true? The LORD said. *You haven't seen him in quite a while. What's more, as you may remember, the last time you saw him you were wrong about some things too, but I've helped you change since then. Why do you assume I haven't helped him change, as well?*

Later, I found out that minister had indeed changed. But like me, he'd assumed I hadn't, so we were both holding something against each other.

If, instead of sitting there in the car bad-mouthing him and talking ugly about his ministry, I had just talked to him, I could have put an end to the strife between us. That would have been

LIVE FEAR FREE

far better. Criticizing him didn't do either of us any good. If I had continued doing it, it would have kept the door open for the devil to come in on that strife and beat our spiritual brains out with it. But I didn't give the devil that opportunity. Right there in the car, I forgave the minister I'd been criticizing and cleaned the strife and unforgiveness out of my spirit.

Since then, I've developed the habit of making forgiveness a daily part of my life.

I encourage you to develop the same habit.

Every day, check your heart for any unforgiveness and strife. If you find any, deal with it immediately by taking the four steps The LORD gave me the day He first taught me how to clean out my spiritual pipe.

Step One: Confess the sin of unforgiveness.

Step Two: Forgive anyone and everyone of anything you have held against them—whether their offenses were big or small— even as God has forgiven you. Don't wait until you feel like it; do it as an act of your will, and do it by faith.

Faith must be involved because forgiving like God does takes supernatural power. When He forgives, He remembers our sins and iniquities no more. (See Hebrews 10:17.) You can't cleanse your consciousness of something someone did to you on your own. God must do that work in you. If you trust Him to do so, He will. Just as He promised in 1 John 1:9, He will cleanse your consciousness of all unrighteousness and all offense toward the person who wronged you.

"But Brother Copeland, can't I wait to forgive until the person asks me to forgive them? Or can't I at least take a few months to work through the forgiveness process?"

When You Stand Praying

No, neither of those things are scriptural. Jesus didn't tell us to take a few months to work on forgiving those we have "ought against." Nor did He tell us to forgive them when they ask us. He told us to do it when we "stand praying" (Mark 11:25).

You're not going to stand there praying for three months. So, obviously it doesn't take that long to forgive. You can do it in one prayer.

Once you forgive, determine to treat those you have forgiven as if they never wronged you. Make a quality decision to not touch that trespass again with your thought life. If you hear someone else who is offended with that person talking badly about them and you join in—even for a moment—correct yourself. Stop and say, "Wait a minute, I should not be talking unkindly about that person. God, forgive me of it right now." Then take the opportunity to pray for them.

If you're in a situation where you continue to have contact with the person you've forgiven, purposely be kind to them. Extend the Love of God to them. Love will bring Jesus in on the situation, and once He's involved, something good is bound to happen.

First, something good will happen in you. Because you kept yourself clean of strife and operated according to God's kingdom principle of Love, you will come out victorious and BLESSED. Second, through your Love and forgiveness, you will open the door for the other person to be BLESSED and changed…and in many instances they will be. I've seen such change happen in a matter of hours. I've also seen it take years. But however long it takes, it's worth the wait.

Step Three: Once you have forgiven anyone who has wronged you, receive your own forgiveness from God. Don't wait until you "feel forgiven" to believe He has forgiven you. Just rejoice by faith

LIVE FEAR FREE

in the knowledge that He has erased the memory of your sin from His consciousness and made you perfectly righteous before Him.

Step Four: Praise and thank God.

That's it! That's how you purge your spiritual pipe of unforgiveness and strife so you can live a faith-filled, fear-free life from now until Jesus returns!

The day The LORD gave me those four steps, He said to me, *What I'm showing you right now will help elevate the Body of Christ in these last days. It will help her ride above the storms of life, and she'll ride that crest right into the resurrection and the portals of glory.*

Love, faith and forgiveness will ultimately capture death itself and render it helpless in our midst!

We've already seen this happen in some cases. Think about Jesus praying on the cross for those who crucified Him, "Father, forgive them; for they know not what they do" (Luke 23:34). His Love, faith and forgiveness triumphed over death, and it could not hold Him. Think about Stephen praying for the people as they were stoning *him,* "LORD, lay not this sin to their charge" (Acts 7:60). He saw the heavens open and beheld Jesus in glory at the right hand of God, standing to receive him.

The people who crucified Jesus didn't kill Him. He laid down His own life and then took it up again in the glory of the Resurrection.

The people throwing the stones didn't kill Stephen. Jesus caught his spirit up before his body died…and gave him a standing ovation.

That's the kind of faith and power that can flow through a forgiving heart! Release it to flow through you by praying this prayer right now:

When You Stand Praying

Dear Heavenly Father, in the Name of Jesus, I confess and repent of the sin of unforgiveness. At this moment, I forgive [name anyone who comes to your mind]. As an act of my will and by faith, I release them from any and all trespasses I have held against them. By Your power, LORD, cleanse my spirit of every memory of every trespass that has been committed against me. I release those trespasses to Your Spirit to be put as far from me as the east is from the west (Psalm 103:12). LORD, I trust You to do the same with the sins I have committed. I believe that right now You forgive me and cleanse me of all unrighteousness. I praise You and thank You, LORD, for forgiving me and setting me free!

CHAPTER 7

THE FEAR-FREE, FAILURE-PROOF LIFE OF LOVE

CHAPTER 7

THE FEAR-FREE, FAILURE-PROOF LIFE OF LOVE

*There is no fear in Love; but perfect Love
casteth out fear: because fear hath torment.
He that feareth is not made perfect in Love.
(1 John 4:18)*

HERE'S SOMETHING I'VE LEARNED ABOUT spiritual revelations: The more important they are, the faster the devil goes to work to try to stop us from acting on them. For example, when I received the revelation about the power of forgiveness and shared it with my staff, the devil wasted no time at all. He immediately started pressuring us to get into strife with one another. As I mentioned in the last chapter, as soon as we committed to operate in forgiveness, we suddenly had more opportunities to fuss with one another than ever before.

I saw the same thing happen when I began to get a revelation of the power and importance of walking in divine Love. I was preparing to preach a series of meetings about it, and the night before the first service...what happened? I got the opportunity to be unloving, and I took it. I got irritated about something and flew off the handle.

LIVE FEAR FREE

Given the timing, I was particularly embarrassed by my reaction. I thought, *Here I am about to minister to people about perfecting their Love walk, and I couldn't even make it to the first service without stepping out of Love myself.*

I repented of course, got back on track, and began preaching the services as planned. On the third night, I asked the congregation, "How many of you have had the opportunity to blow your stack and be anything but loving since these meetings started?" Their reaction told the story. Nearly everyone raised a hand.

I knew right then, if satan is that fiercely opposed to us walking in Love, it must be extremely dangerous to his agenda. So, from that point on, I determined to do what the Apostle Paul said in 1 Corinthians 14:1: *"Eagerly pursue* and seek to acquire [this] Love [make it your aim, your great quest]" *(Amplified Bible, Classic Edition).* I also determined to keep preaching about it, because I am fiercely in favor of anything that's dangerous to the devil, and nothing is more dangerous to him than Love.

Why is Love such a threat to him?

Because he uses the spiritual force of fear to control people, and as 1 John 4:18 says: "There is no fear in Love, but perfect Love casts out fear" *(New King James Version).*

Operating in perfected Love is different from simply *having* Love. All of us, as believers, *have* Love because the moment we were born again, the Love of God was "shed abroad in our hearts by the Holy Ghost" (Romans 5:5). But the fact that we have Love isn't what the devil is worried about. What he is desperate to do is to stop the Love we have from being perfected.

Perfected Love is Love that is *developed and brought to completion.* It functions in our lives as we feed on God's WORD, fellowship with Him, and let His Love flow through us to others.

122

The Fear-Free, Failure-Proof Life of Love

When perfected Love is in operation in us, by its own power, it rids us of fear and causes our faith to work as God designed (Galatians 5:5). It frees us to walk in faith as naturally as unbelievers walk in fear.

Unbelievers don't have to try to work up fear, do they? No, it's normal for them.

When it comes to faith, the same should be true for those who are born again. Believing God ought to be normal for us. We shouldn't have to try to "work up" faith in His WORD. Our faith ought to be always at the ready—and the more we allow the Love of God to develop in us, the more it will be!

"But Brother Copeland, sometimes I just don't feel very loving."

That's true for all of us, at times. But it doesn't matter, because for us, as believers, Love is not a feeling. Love is a Person. God is Love.

Faith is something God *has*. It's something He *uses*. But Love is who He *is*. So we love not by focusing on our feelings, but by looking to Him. We love by looking in His WORD at how He loves and following His example as well-beloved children imitate their father. (See Ephesians 5:1, *Amplified Bible, Classic Edition.*)

In the Gospels, we can see in Jesus what Love looks like in human form! He is the express image of the Father (Hebrews 1:3), so He is Love just as God is Love. When He came to earth as a man, He was "touched with the feeling of our infirmities" and "was in all points tempted like as we are" (Hebrews 4:15). Therefore He, too, must have had times when He didn't feel very loving.

Yet He never sinned! No matter how He felt, Jesus continued to walk in Love. And by looking at how He did it, we can see how to do it, too.

LIVE FEAR FREE

MOVED BY COMPASSION HIMSELF

Consider, for example, the time Jesus found out that John the Baptist had been murdered. That must have been extremely hard on Jesus' emotions. The Bible doesn't specifically tell us how He felt but, in His humanity, He must have felt anything but warm and loving upon hearing how brutally and senselessly John had been killed.

After all, John the Baptist was Jesus' cousin! Just six months apart in age, they were close to one another both as family and in ministry. No one else in Jesus' family understood His ministry and calling like John did.

Even as a baby, John had leapt in his mother's womb when Mary told her Aunt Elizabeth that she was going to bear the Messiah. After he began his own ministry, John was the one who had prepared the way for Jesus and announced to the crowds that He was coming. He'd been the first to declare, when Jesus came to be baptized in water, "Behold the Lamb of God, which taketh away the sin of the world" (John 1:29). And he was the one who had seen the Holy Spirit come down on Jesus like a dove and remain on Him.

Jesus' relationship with John was precious to Him. Jesus held him in such high esteem that He publicly acknowledged him as the greatest prophet ever born of a woman.

Rather than being honored, however, as the great prophet that he was, John ended up being arrested like a common criminal. His so-called crime? Saying that King Herod's immoral relationship with Herodias, his brother's wife, was unlawful.

Because the Jews believed John was a prophet, Herod didn't initially intend to kill him. He just planned to keep him in prison.

The Fear-Free, Failure-Proof Life of Love

But when Herod's birthday was kept, the daughter of Herodias danced before them, and pleased Herod. Whereupon he promised with an oath to give her whatsoever she would ask. And she, being before instructed of her mother, said, Give me here John Baptist's head in a charger. And the king was sorry: nevertheless for the oath's sake, and them which sat with him at meat, he commanded it to be given her. And he sent, and beheaded John in the prison. And his head was brought in a charger, and given to the damsel: and she brought it to her mother. And his disciples came, and took up the body, and buried it, and went and told Jesus (Matthew 14:6–12).

Put yourself in Jesus' position for a moment. Think about what it must have been like for Him to hear that the only man on earth who truly understood what He was called to do, a man He loved and who was part of His family, had been so cruelly butchered. That his head had been cut off and brought into a drunken orgy on a plate, just because an immoral ruler had gotten excited by a woman's dance and said something stupid.

What a mockery that would be! How would you react to that kind of news?

Probably the same way Jesus did. He initially reacted by trying to get away from everyone. Apparently desiring to go somewhere where He could be alone, "He departed thence by ship into a desert place apart" (verse 13). The multitudes who continually surrounded Him, however, found out where He had gone. So they followed Him there on foot out of the cities.

At that point, Jesus could have understandably been angry and exasperated. He could have said, "Can't you people give Me some space? Can't I at least have some time to Myself to deal with My feelings about this horrible thing that has happened in My family?"

LIVE FEAR FREE

Jesus could even have used those people to get some revenge on Herod. Since the working-class Jews who flocked to Jesus didn't like Herod anyway, He could have incited them to revolt. He could have decided, *I've had all the debauchery and violence from this immoral king and his illegal wife that I'm going to take,* and said, "Let's go after him, guys!"

But that's not what Jesus did. Even though He was personally hurting, He was not moved by His own human emotions. Instead, when He saw the great multitude, He "was moved with compassion toward them, and he healed their sick" (verse 14).

I used to wonder why Jesus responded this way rather than retaliating. But I eventually realized He *did* retaliate—just not against people. You see, He understood that people weren't His real enemy. Herod wasn't his real enemy. Neither was Herodias or her daughter who asked for the head of John the Baptist. They were all being manipulated and controlled by satan.

If Jesus had lashed out against the people involved in that situation, He would have been doing exactly what satan wanted. He would have destroyed His ministry. His mission of Love would have been aborted and satan would have won. So, instead of going after Herod, Jesus retaliated against satan directly.

Moved by compassion, He healed the sick.

Don't you know healing the multitudes was satisfying to Jesus that day? Sickness and disease are works of the devil! By healing the sick, Jesus hit satan where it hurt the most. He didn't just strike at the surface of that murderous situation. He struck its very root by allowing Himself to be moved by compassion.

Notice, the Bible doesn't say Jesus was moved by a "feeling" of compassion. No, He was moved by Compassion Himself. He was moved by God. That's why He didn't lash out at people. He

126

The Fear-Free, Failure-Proof Life of Love

knew He was on a mission to love and redeem them. "For God sent not his Son into the world to condemn the world; but that the world through him might be saved" (John 3:17).

As believers, you and I have been sent by Jesus to carry out the same mission. We're His representatives on earth, here to tell people about Him, love them and minister to them like He did. Even in the most difficult situations, we're to be moved by Compassion Himself instead of by our own feelings and physical senses.

If you're thinking that's easier said than done, you're right—especially when the devil uses people to come against us. Responding to them in Love can be hard. But then, war is always hard, and, as believers, if we're living in this world, we're in a war. It's not a war against flesh and blood. As we know and must remember, it's a spiritual war against satan, his principalities, powers, rulers of the darkness of this world and spiritual wickedness in high places (Ephesians 6:12).

> For though we walk in the flesh, we do not war after the flesh: (For the weapons of our warfare are not carnal, but mighty through God to the pulling down of strong holds;) casting down imaginations, and every high thing that exalteth itself against the knowledge of God, and bringing into captivity every thought to the obedience of Christ (2 Corinthians 10:3-5).

Bringing our thoughts into captivity to Christ means bringing our thought life, speech and actions into alignment with Compassion Himself. It means we react in the midst of every battle the way Love reacts and not according to our carnal senses. No matter how ugly people may act toward us, we don't fight them. We love people and fight the devil, just as Jesus did.

LIVE FEAR FREE

As He Is, So Are We in This World

"But I'm not Jesus!" you might say. "I can't be loving all the time like He was, and I certainly can't do the things He did. I don't have that kind of supernatural power."

On His own, Jesus didn't have that kind of power either when He was on earth. He said Himself, "The Father that dwelleth in me, he doeth the works" (John 14:10). What's more, Jesus said just before He turned His ministry over to us as His disciples, "He that believeth on me, the works that I do shall he do also; and greater works than these shall he do; because I go unto my Father" (verse 12).

In other words, according to Jesus, you, as a believer, have available to you the same power He had available to Him when He was on earth. You have the Father dwelling in you just as He did. And just as the Father revealed His Love for people by doing supernatural works of Love through Jesus, now the Father intends to do the same through you.

This has been God's kingdom-building plan for more than 2,000 years. The only problem has been that the devil has all too often managed to scare believers out of putting it into operation. Using unscriptural religious attitudes to frighten and intimidate them, he's managed to convince many Christians that John 14:12 doesn't apply to them. He's told them they're too ordinary to do Jesus' works.

The devil has even talked some into believing that the day of miracles and healing the sick has passed away. That those things ceased when the early apostles died, and no longer happen today.

Such thinking isn't anything new. It's the kind of thinking that stopped the people of Nazareth from receiving from Jesus. When

The Fear-Free, Failure-Proof Life of Love

He read Isaiah 61:1-2[5] to them and said, "This day is this scripture fulfilled in your ears" (Luke 4:2), they must have thought, *Now wait a minute here! Those verses were about the Messiah. They were written in Isaiah's day. They couldn't possibly apply to someone from our little town, right now, today.*

They were wrong, of course, and so are people who think that way today.

What Jesus said about believers doing His works could not possibly have just applied to only a few special saints. It could not possibly be that healing and miracles passed away with the last apostle. If that were the case, it would mean the apostles healed and worked miracles by their own power—and they didn't!

Just like Jesus, the apostles ministered by the power of the Father who dwelled within them—and the indwelling power of the Father, the Holy Spirit, is still around! He hasn't passed away anywhere. He came on the Church in Acts 2 on the Day of Pentecost and never left. He's still here today, living in every born-again believer, helping each of us do the works of Jesus and walk in His perfected Love.

One way the Holy Spirit helps us is by bringing God's WORD to our remembrance. For as 1 John 2:5 says, "Whoso keepeth His WORD, in him verily is the Love of God perfected." We can't walk in God's perfected Love by following after carnal ideas and the sentimental stuff the world calls love. We can only love like God does by putting His WORD first place, believing it and acting on it.

When you think about it, this makes perfect sense. God and His WORD are One, and He is Love. So, when you're acting

---

5 "The Spirit of The LORD God is upon me; because The LORD hath anointed me to preach good tidings unto the meek; he hath sent me to bind up the brokenhearted, to proclaim liberty to the captives, and the opening of the prison to them that are bound; to proclaim the acceptable year of The LORD..." (Isaiah 61:1-2).

LIVE FEAR FREE

on The WORD, you're walking in Love. You're being moved by Compassion.

As you do what Compassion said to do (whether you feel like it or not) the Love of God is perfected in your life, and you can walk without fear because Love does not fail. Let me say that again: *Love does not fail!* It *can't* fail because God can't fail. You can't fail when you're operating in it because you're operating according to God's WORD, and God always backs His WORD. He always sees to it that His WORD is upheld, and that failure does not occur.

None of the world's so-called secrets of success can make you failure-proof. But the WORD and Love of God can do exactly that. So, in these perilous, unpredictable last days, become WORD-and-Love-of-God minded!

Develop your awareness of the Love of God that's been shed abroad in your heart by the Holy Spirit. Meditate on the fact that Love Himself is in you. Dig into The WORD and find out: How does Love think? How does Love behave? What does Love do and not do? How does Love respond?

One passage of Scripture that will help you answer those questions is 1 Corinthians 13:4-8. I recommend studying those verses in the *Amplified Bible, Classic Edition* and turning them into a faith confession. Substitute the word *I* for the word *Love* and practice saying:

> I endure long and am patient and kind; I never am envious, nor do I boil over with jealousy. I am not boastful or vainglorious, and do not display myself haughtily. I am not conceited (arrogant and inflated with pride); I am not rude (unmannerly) and do not act unbecomingly. I do not insist on my own rights or my own way, for I am

not self-seeking. I am not touchy or fretful or resentful. I take no account of the evil done to me [I pay no attention to a suffered wrong]. I do not rejoice at injustice and unrighteousness, but rejoice when right and truth prevail. I bear up under anything and everything that comes, I am ever ready to believe the best of every person, my hopes are fadeless under all circumstances, and I endure everything [without weakening]. I walk in Love, so I never fail.

Talk about positioning yourself to walk in the power of the Holy Spirit! As you operate in Love according to God's WORD, not only are you yielded to Him, His power is yielded to you. There's no strife between you and Him. You are in complete harmony with Him. You're taking every step with Him, and He's taking every step with you. So when the Holy Spirit moves on you to release the mighty, miracle-working power of God in the face of some devilish situation, you stand ready. Even in the face of the most impossible odds, you'll do what Divine Compassion and the Holy Spirit tell you to do, because you know that Love never fails.

Years ago, I was preaching a series of meetings at a little church in a remote area of Jamaica, and the pastor's eighteen-year-old granddaughter died while the church service was going on. She was in her family's house alone, on the mountainside above the church, when it happened. So, no one knew until after the meeting when her mother and father found her slumped over the table, dead.

Born with a rheumatic heart, she'd been told by her family all her life to be careful. "Remember, baby, you have a bad heart," they said. "You could just fall down dead any minute." They'd all lived in fear of it for years. Although they were precious Spirit-filled believers, they didn't know any better because they didn't know The WORD. That's why I was there.

LIVE FEAR FREE

The pastor found out I was preaching at another church in the region and asked me to come preach to his congregation as well.

"We've been fasting and praying for over a year for God to send us someone with some revelation knowledge," he said. "We want to know about faith and The WORD of God."

That evening, I had just finished the service and was walking up the pathway to their house where I was staying, when I heard the girl's mother screaming from the front room, "My baby is dead! My baby is dead!" By then I'd reached the bottom step of the stairway that led up to the house. It was long and steep because the house sat about twenty feet above the path.

Although I'd walked up and down all those stairs many times since I'd been there, I have absolutely no mental recollection of climbing them that night. I don't know how I got to the top. All I know is that the power of God came on me, and when I put my foot on the first step, my next step was on the front porch.

Once inside the house, I saw the pastor's granddaughter cradled in her daddy's arms. Her head was on his chest, and he was standing there holding her, wide-eyed in shock. Taking her lifeless hand in mine, I could tell she'd died earlier in the evening. Her body had already cooled off and begun to stiffen. Gripped by the compassion of God, I stopped for a moment and inquired of The LORD. He told me exactly what to do, and I did it.

I said to that young girl, "I speak life to you in the Name of Jesus."

Nothing happened, so I said it again, "I speak life to you in the Name of Jesus."

Still, no response. But Love never fails, so I said again, "In the Name of Jesus whose I am and whom I serve, I speak life to you NOW!"

The Fear-Free, Failure-Proof Life of Love

She suddenly lurched and opened her eyes.

"Oh!" she said. Then looking up into the face of her father, who was still in shock, she said, "Papa?"

Hallelujah! Those are the kinds of things Jesus did when He was on earth, and according to the New Testament, they're the kinds of things every believer ought to do. As 1 John says:

> He that saith he abideth in him ought himself also so to walk, even as he walked…. Herein is our Love made perfect, that we may have boldness in the day of judgment: because as he is, so are we in this world. There is no fear in Love; but perfect Love casteth out fear: because fear hath torment. He that feareth is not made perfect in Love (1 John 2:6, 4:17-18).

Notice, those verses don't say as Jesus *was,* so are we in this world. They say, "as He *is,* so are we in this world." This is the reason perfected Love makes us fearless. When we walk in it, we become aware that we are as Jesus *is*—right now, today.

Where is Jesus today? He is seated at "the right hand of the Majesty on high" (Hebrews 1:3). Can you imagine Him being afraid of anything from that vantage point? Can you imagine Jesus, in His exalted position at the right hand of the Father, worrying about whether He's going to have enough to see us through whatever challenges arise in these last days?

Certainly not!

God has given Jesus His whole kingdom! All authority both in heaven and on earth has been given to Him! He has at His disposal more than enough of everything to make sure that we don't lack anything. He is well able to provide each of us personally and the Church, as a whole, with more than we can ask or even think.

LIVE FEAR FREE

And it's not just according to the limited resources of earth but, as Philippians 4:19 says, "according to His riches in glory."

GIVING IS IN YOUR SPIRITUAL DNA

God's riches in glory are inexhaustible. You will never have to say to Him, "I know finances are tight in heaven right now. I understand You're in a recession up there, but I need some assistance with my bills this month. Do You think You could afford to help me out a little down here?"

No, you'd never talk to God like that. It would be ridiculous. He lives in a city with jeweled walls and pearl gates. His streets are made of gold so refined it's transparent. He has more than enough to supply not only *your* need according to His riches in glory, but to provide you with plenty to give to others.

What's more, that's His clear intention.

He's a giver! He "so loved the world, that he gave..." (John 3:16). So, as you love like He does, you will give too, and He will help you. First, He will supply you with something to give. Then, as you start giving, He'll keep multiplying and supplying you with more of whatever you gave.

Jesus said, "Give, and it shall be given unto you; good measure, pressed down, and shaken together, and running over, shall men give into your bosom. For with the same measure that ye mete withal it shall be measured to you again" (Luke 6:38). That means if you give of your finances to help get the gospel to people or to help meet their material needs, God will increase you financially. If you give to the sick by ministering healing to them in Jesus' Name, He will keep furnishing you with more power to get them healed.

Of course, if you give financially just so people will notice

134

The Fear-Free, Failure-Proof Life of Love

you, or you start praying for the sick just to build yourself a big ministry, that's different. In that case, God is not obliged to keep you supplied, and eventually you won't have enough. Selfishness will draw you off course, allowing satan to operate in your affairs and make you ineffective.

But if you'll start giving to people and praying for the sick because you love them, God will provide you with more than enough to do for them what Love demands.

The life of the giver is wonderful! It will do more for you than you ever dreamed.

One person who famously found this out was the well-known American business magnate, John D. Rockefeller. Although he was one of the richest men in the world, before he started giving in 1897, he was virtually a walking dead man. His stomach was so ruined with ulcers that, at only fifty years old, the doctors told him he wouldn't live more than another five years.

Unable to eat much more than milk-soaked crackers and faced with what appeared to be a death sentence, Mr. Rockefeller considered how to spend the few years he had left to live. He had already been everywhere he wanted to go. He'd seen as much of the world as he wanted to see, and bought and sold everything he wanted to buy and sell.

What can I do that I haven't already done? he wondered.

The answer, he realized, was *give*. So, he decided that before he died, he would give away all his money.

As it turned out, however, this proved to be impossible. The more money he gave, the more money he made. He couldn't get rid of it fast enough. He kept trying, though, and in the process his stomach healed up. He went on to live to the age of

LIVE FEAR FREE

ninety-seven, and is still recognized today as one of the world's most generous givers, ever.

Believers ought to be the world's most generous givers, too! Like Mr. Rockefeller, we have good reason to make that our goal. Our reason is Jesus! We give because of what He has given to us.

He gave *Himself* for us, not when we were righteous but when we were at our worst. He laid down His life and shed His precious blood for us when we were unworthy sinners. He gave, and is still giving, us everything He is and everything He has.

Jesus is the ultimate Giver, and when we begin to love and give like He does, we begin to live life in His style—without fear of what satan can do to us, without fear of what man can do to us, and without fear of the curse.

"But I can't afford to give," someone might say.

You can't afford not to! For one thing, it's the most exciting, fulfilling adventure ever. For another, as a born-again believer, loving and giving is in your spiritual DNA. It's who you are and what you're here on earth to do.

As Jesus is, so are you in this world! You are His epistle, or letter, written by Him for the world to read.

People who don't even own Bibles can see and experience the Love of Jesus through you. As you gird yourself with Love and serve the unworthy and the selfish, it's as if Jesus Himself is serving them. It's as if the very blood of the Lamb flows again and again as you love the unlovely and give your life for them.

You and I, as believers, don't give our lives for people by literally dying on a cross. Jesus has already done that. We give our lives by developing every ability and talent God has given us so

The Fear-Free, Failure-Proof Life of Love

that we may be of benefit to those who have no ability. We give our lives on our knees in intercession, praying for other people.

We give our lives by seeking out ways to give financially and BLESS those who can do nothing for us in return. By extending kindness even to those who are unkind to us, and by living in such a way that the neighbor next door, who has wondered if God cares about him, can look at us and realize the answer is yes, God cares.

Oh, dear believer, this is *God's* life! This is His way of living. When you live His way, He will pour His resources through you. He will multiply you supernaturally, and you'll experience in your own life what the little boy in Luke 9 experienced when He gave Jesus his lunch of loaves and fish to feed the hungry multitudes.

That little boy is a good example of someone who could have said, "I can't afford to give." He had just enough food for himself that day, but he gave it to Jesus, who BLESSED it. He took the little boy's basket of food, put it in the hands of the disciples and, as they distributed it, it increased. It kept multiplying until thousands of people "were all filled: and there was taken up of fragments that remained to them twelve baskets" (Luke 9:17).

This is the kind of thing our Jesus can do, and He is the One who is backing your giving! As you give Him what you have—even if right now it's just a little—He'll not only turn it into enough to BLESS others, He will fill and multiply your baskets and bank accounts. He will "open you the windows of heaven, and pour you out a BLESSING, that *there shall* not *be room* enough *to receive it*" (Malachi 3:10).

This is God's plan for the last-days Church! We're not to be just a social organization, doling out what we can to meet a few needs. No, in these final hours before Jesus returns, when people in darkness are increasingly desperate, we're to show them that

LIVE FEAR FREE

God loves them and that He is their Answer. We're to let them see, coming through our hands, the abundant life, Love and BLESSING of The LORD Jesus Christ.

As I was preaching about these things years ago, the Holy Spirit gave me this prophetic word:

There is available to My people, saith The LORD, *a method of giving, an operating of pouring out of My Spirit to others as I pour out of My Spirit upon you. And in that place, there is no lack. In that place, there is no depression and no inflation. When the prices go up, I pour out more,* saith The LORD. *They'll not catch you short. They'll not catch you without. They'll not catch you with an area of doubt or unbelief.*

If you'll busy yourself—I repeat, busy yourself—at the art of learning how to give in My Name, you will not have time to be in doubt and unbelief, and I will pour financial resources toward you. I will pour businesses into your hands. I will cause men in these last days to raise up businesses and industries that men don't even know about yet, because I am the Author of all natural resources.

I am the Author of meeting every need. Everything was created for and by Me. I will bring it to pass and raise up industries for the single purpose of BLESSING people who have determined to give. I will do it, saith God, *and no one can stop Me. And those same people will preach this gospel and walk in and among people and diseases shall fall off their bodies and blind eyes shall be opened, and men that have never spoken shall speak. And you shall see the glory of The LORD when you begin to set yourself as givers and walk in the Love life, for this is My walk. And when you and I are in agreement,* saith The LORD, *who then can stop us?*

CHAPTER 8

UNDER THE PROTECTIVE UMBRELLA OF GOD

CHAPTER 8

UNDER THE PROTECTIVE UMBRELLA OF GOD

*What then shall we say to [all] this? If God is for us, who [can be]
against us? [Who can be our foe, if God is on our side?]
(Romans 8:31, AMPLIFIED BIBLE, CLASSIC EDITION)*

I'VE NEVER BEEN COMPLETELY SATISFIED just to know that
something works. I've always wanted to know how and why.
Even as a little boy, I wasn't content to just look at the clock
on the nightstand beside my bed to see what time it was. I had to
take it apart and see what made it tick. The fact that I never managed to get the clock put back together again didn't do anything
to change my mindset, either. That's still the way I think.

So when I found out that "perfect Love casteth out fear"
(1 John 4:18), I immediately wanted to know why. After fellowshipping with The LORD over the question, I got the revelation:
Love casts out fear because Love is the opposite of selfishness—
and selfishness is the foundation of fear!

If I have a fear of man, for instance, it's because I'm focused
on myself. I'm afraid of what others might do to me or think
about me. I'm not afraid of others because I care about them. I'm

LIVE FEAR FREE

not going to fear you for your sake. No, if I'm afraid of you it's because I have *me* on my mind.

That's true for all of us. It's one of the reasons fear came so naturally to us before we were born again. Until we received Jesus, like all human beings, we were self-centered. We couldn't be otherwise because we had a fallen, sinful nature. Selfishness was literally bred into us.

By the time we were toddlers, we could act selfishly without even having to think about it. If another child picked up one of our toys, we instinctively grabbed it back and said, "Mine!" As we grew, our toys and our ways of fighting others over them may have become more sophisticated, but until we responded to the gospel, our motive in life remained the same: to look out for number one—*me*.

What result did that motive produce?

Sin.

Sin is always the result when our motive is selfishness.

Now that we have been born again, however, our motive in life can change. Because we've become new creations with a new nature, we're not bound to self-centeredness and sin anymore. The Love of God has been shed abroad in our hearts by the Holy Spirit, and His Love isn't like natural human love, which is possessive and self-focused. His Love motivates us to give, and to focus on being a BLESSING to others.

What's more, unlike selfishness, which is the foundation of fear, the Love of God is the foundation of faith! It sets us free to believe and do what God says in His WORD.

When I began learning to operate in the Love of God, I found a whole new kind of freedom because I got *me* off my hands. I

Under the Protective Umbrella of God

realized I don't have to spend my life just looking out for myself anymore. Because I know God loves me and will look out for me, I can live to give without having to be afraid of anything or anyone—not the curse, not satan, not God and not man.

- I don't have to be afraid of the curse of the Law because the Love of God has broken that curse for me
- I don't have to be afraid of satan because the Love of God operating through Christ Jesus has defeated satan and rendered him powerless over me
- I don't have to have an unjustified fear of God because He is a perfectly loving Father, and I am His dearly beloved child
- I don't have to fear man because God loves me and is for me; and as Romans 8:31 says, if God is for me, none can stand against me.

Knowing that if I'm walking with God in faith and Love, none can stand against me, frees me from having to push people away or push them around to make sure I come out on top in every situation. Instead of fighting or avoiding people, I can just love them, do for them whatever God tells me, and trust Him to take care of me.

In other words, I can obey the command Jesus gave in Luke 6:27-29: "Love your enemies, do good to those who hate you, BLESS those who curse you, and pray for those who spitefully use you. To him who strikes you on the one cheek, offer the other also..." *(New King James Version)*.

"Well," someone might say, "I've never understood that turn-the-other-cheek business. If I do that, people will walk all over me."

No, they won't. They might try but they'll fail because when

LIVE FEAR FREE

you turn the other cheek in Love and by faith, you activate a spiritual principle that will protect you.

The carnal world doesn't understand this principle. Neither do many Christians. But it's very powerful. It will supernaturally protect and deliver you from people and situations that you would be helpless against in the natural.

You can see an example of this principle at work in the life of Jesus when He preached in Nazareth. It was only because of God's supernatural protection that He got out of there alive. As I mentioned in the last chapter, when He announced to the congregation that He had come to fulfill the prophecy in Isaiah 61, they really got riled up. They didn't just strike Him on the cheek; they "were filled with wrath, and rose up, and thrust him out of the city, and led him unto the brow of the hill whereon their city was built, that they might cast him down headlong" (Luke 4:28-29).

Jesus hadn't done anything to those people except love them! He hadn't lifted a finger against them or talked ugly to them. He had just preached to them from the written WORD of God, and they responded by trying to kill Him. They physically pushed Him to the edge of a cliff, intending to throw Him to His death.

It's a good thing Jesus' disciples weren't with Him that day. They wouldn't have been in favor of turning the other cheek in that situation. They would have wanted to call for "fire to come down from heaven, and consume" those people. We know they would because that's what they wanted to do in Samaria when the people there refused to receive Jesus (Luke 9:54).

In Samaria, Jesus rebuked the disciples and told them they didn't know what manner of spirit they were of. "The Son of man is not come to destroy men's lives, but to save them," He said (verses 55-56). Jesus never dealt with people who acted ugly toward Him by fighting and doing them harm.

144

Under the Protective Umbrella of God

So, in Nazareth, rather than doubling up His fist and slugging the people who were shoving him toward the cliff, He practiced what He preached. He turned the other cheek and "passing through their midst, He went on His way" (Luke 4:30, *Amplified Bible, Classic Edition*).

Think about that! Jesus walked right through the middle of the crowd and went on about His business. He didn't even have to push anyone aside to get away. No one could touch Him!

That wasn't just the case in Nazareth, it was true throughout Jesus' life. People opposed Him and plotted against Him all through His ministry, but no one could harm Him until the time came for Him to go to the Cross. Even then, His persecutors couldn't do anything to Him without His permission. They could only crucify Him because He let them.

At any point, from His arrest to His crucifixion, Jesus could have prayed and "more than twelve legions of angels" would have been sent to protect Him (Matthew 26:53). But instead, He allowed Himself to be nailed to the Cross. He chose to step out by faith from under the umbrella of God's protection so that the plan of God could be fulfilled.

As He said in John 10, "I lay down my life, that I might take it again. No man taketh it from me, but I lay it down of myself. I have power to lay it down, and I have power to take it again" (verses 17-18).

TURNING A FIGHT INTO A TESTIMONY

When I was first born again, I didn't know anything about God's umbrella of protection, so the concept of turning the other cheek was foreign to me. Growing up, I had been so high tempered that if someone ever took a swing at me, I hit him back

LIVE FEAR FREE

hard and fast. My motto back then was always: *Hit him now, talk later.* That's the way a carnal man thinks. I figured I had to operate like that to live.

It wasn't easy for me to get over that way of thinking. Even after I received Jesus as my LORD, I found myself wanting to physically react and retaliate when someone did me wrong. I managed to restrain myself, but I would still get mad enough to want to fight.

As I kept studying God's WORD, though, I began to see that if we do what He says, we can expect the miraculous to happen. So, I asked The LORD one day, "What can I expect to happen when I turn the other cheek?"

You can expect the man who's taking a swing at you to not be able to hit you, He said.

That changed my perspective! It made turning the other cheek sound a lot more exciting. After all, anybody can fight, but not just anyone can stand in front of someone who's throwing punches and not get hit. That takes faith. It turns a fight into a testimony!

One of the first times I personally saw this happen, I was preaching in Hereford, Texas. I had been holding meetings there for several weeks in an abandoned drugstore we had rented. One evening as I was ministering, a great big, angry-looking fellow came charging in the door and headed straight toward me.

Even though I was standing on the makeshift platform our ministry team had built, which stood several inches above the floor, the man stood taller than me. Built like a linebacker, he also looked to be much stronger. I didn't know exactly what he had in mind. But as he barreled toward the platform, I just stood there looking at him.

Under the Protective Umbrella of God

"Jesus," I said quietly, "here he comes."

Right before he reached the platform, the man stopped and pointed his finger at me. Frowning fiercely, he started to speak but all he managed to say in English was, "I'll tell you…." Then he began speaking in other tongues. Looking shocked and bewildered, he slapped his hand over his mouth. After being quiet for a few moments, he tried again to say what he had intended, but again all he could do was speak in tongues. Finally, he just ducked his head in embarrassment and walked out.

I found out later the man had once been a truck driver and an alcoholic. God had delivered him from alcohol, called him to preach, and he'd become the pastor of a local Methodist church. He was upset because some of his members had come to my meetings and received the Baptism in the Holy Spirit. He had also heard that I had preached what he considered to be heresy. I had said that after Jesus was crucified, He went to hell in our place to pay the full spiritual price for our sin.

The very idea of someone saying Jesus went to hell made this Methodist pastor downright mad! So, he came into the service that night to set me straight. Before he could start in on me though, Jesus intervened and baptized him with the Holy Spirit.

The next day, the man came back to see me.

"Copeland, I apologize," he said. "After I left the service last night, I couldn't sleep. So, I went over to the church, dropped to my knees, and just started talking in tongues. It was so good! After a while, I stopped and said, 'Jesus, did You go to hell?' He said, 'You better believe it, big boy. If I hadn't, you would've.'"

I'm so glad I just stood there when that man came at me, and let Jesus take care of the situation! If I had jumped off the platform and tried to deal with it myself, I would have made a mess

LIVE FEAR FREE

of things. We could have set believers in that town against each other and harmed the whole community.

That's probably what the devil had planned. But Jesus took what he meant for evil and turned it into good. He took what could have been a fight and turned it into a marvelous testimony.

Some years later, in another one of our meetings, something similar happened in the face of a much more dangerous threat. A man in one of our meetings attempted to stab me. In that instance, the Holy Spirit came to my defense before I even knew the man was there. I would have never known about him at all, had his attack not been caught on camera.

On the videotape of the meeting, he could be seen standing in the prayer line with people who had come forward for ministry. When I got within his reach, he raised his knife over me as I was praying for someone. I didn't see it. I didn't feel it either, because before the knife could touch me, the man holding it dropped to the ground like a sack of potatoes.

The video producer saw it happen and could hardly believe his eyes. Astonished, he replayed it over and over. No matter how many times he watched the tape, he could see no visible reason for the man to fall to the ground the moment he raised the knife.

There was just one explanation. The protective power of God went into operation and turned an attack into a miracle.

"But Brother Copeland," you might say, "what about all the attacks that came against the Apostle Paul during his ministry? Why didn't God's protective power work for him?"

It did!

People tried to kill Paul repeatedly, and they repeatedly failed. His persecutors devised one murderous plot after another to stop

Under the Protective Umbrella of God

him from preaching the gospel. But time and again, Paul either escaped their attacks altogether or came through them alive and well enough to go right on ministering. According to the book of Acts, he was delivered from death in city after city.

For instance, in Damascus, when the religious leaders were "guarding the [city's] gates day and night to kill him," their plan was made known to Paul, and "his disciples took him at night and let him down through the [city's] wall, lowering him in a basket or hamper" (Acts 9:24-25, *Amplified Bible, Classic Edition).* He walked away without even having to put up a fight and continued preaching.

In Iconium, when some people made plans to stone him, once again, Paul and his fellow minister, Barnabas, "aware of the situation, made their escape" (Acts 14:6, *Amplified Bible, Classic Edition)* and went to preach in Lystra.

In Lystra, Paul's persecutors actually did manage to stone him. They even "dragged him out of the town, thinking that he was dead. But the disciples formed a circle about him, and he got up and went back into the town" (verses 19-20, *Amplified Bible, Classic Edition).* The next day, he was well enough to travel to another city and continue to preach!

In Jerusalem, the religious rulers became so determined to get rid of Paul that a group of them vowed not to eat or drink until they had killed him. But Paul's nephew got word of their plan, and it was thwarted. Eventually, when Paul was being taken prisoner to Rome, the devil tried and failed to kill him in a shipwreck. Afterward, when the ship's crew decided to kill all the prisoners on board, once again, Paul was protected. The centurion on the ship stopped the soldiers from carrying out their plan because he liked Paul!

LIVE FEAR FREE

You might be thinking, *Yes, but in the end, Paul did wind up being killed by the Romans.*

Not until he knew he had finished the work God had called him to do. When that time came, Paul *chose* to lay down his life and did it gladly. But he did it only when he was ready to depart this life and go to be with Jesus.

How do we know this? Because before he finally decided he was ready to depart, he wrote to the church at Philippi:

> For to me, to live is Christ, and to die is gain. But if I live on in the flesh, this will mean fruit from my labor; yet what I shall choose I cannot tell. For I am hard-pressed between the two, having a desire to depart and be with Christ, which is far better. Nevertheless to remain in the flesh is more needful for you. And being confident of this, I know that I shall remain and continue with you all for your progress and joy of faith (Philippians 1:21–25, *New King James Version*).

When the Apostle Paul penned those words, although he desired to go on to heaven, he realized he needed to remain on the earth to finish his ministry. So, he chose to stay a while longer. But once he knew he had accomplished his mission, he decided he was free to go. He wrote: "I am now ready to be offered, and the time of my departure is at hand. I have fought a good fight, I have finished my course, I have kept the faith" (2 Timothy 4:6-7).

"But didn't Paul suffer physical hardships and persecutions in the course of his ministry?" you might ask.

Yes. He himself acknowledged: "Five times I received from [the hands of] the Jews forty [lashes all] but one; three times I have been beaten with rods; once I was stoned" (2 Corinthians

11:24-25, *Amplified Bible, Classic Edition).* But Paul willingly accepted those difficulties as part of his apostolic calling. Jesus had warned him from the start that preaching the gospel to its fiercest opponents would involve some suffering, and it did.

The persecutions he endured, however, did not accomplish what their perpetrators intended. They temporarily touched his body, but they never touched or wounded his spirit and soul. And they certainly did not stop Paul from fulfilling his commission. On the contrary, Paul said that even though "the Holy Spirit testifies in every city, saying that chains and tribulations await me. But none of these things move me; nor do I count my life dear to myself, so that I may finish my race with joy, and the ministry which I received from The LORD Jesus, to testify to the gospel of the grace of God" (Acts 20:23-24, *New King James Version).*

Notice, Paul didn't just finish his race, he finished it with joy! He even rejoiced over the persecution he and his ministry companions experienced: "We do not become discouraged.... For our light, momentary affliction (this slight distress of the passing hour) is ever more and more abundantly preparing and producing and achieving for us an everlasting weight of glory [beyond all measure, excessively surpassing all comparisons and all calculations, a vast and transcendent glory and BLESSEDNESS never to cease!]" (2 Corinthians 4:17, *Amplified Bible, Classic Edition).*

LOVING HARD-TO-LOVE PEOPLE

The Apostle Paul's compassion and freedom from the fear of man enabled him to turn the other cheek and boldly preach the gospel—even to those who hated, threatened and plotted to kill him. It freed him to boldly go wherever The LORD led and do whatever He said to do. As a result, he left behind him so many changed lives that the world was never the same again.

LIVE FEAR FREE

You can do the same in your world. You don't have to be an apostle like Paul to change people's lives. You just have to be a believer. Jesus said, "He that believeth on me, the works that I do shall he do also; and greater works than these shall he do..." (John 14:12).

Often when we think about the works of Jesus, we think in terms of healing and preaching. But the greatest work of Jesus you can ever do is to love people—especially the unlovely ones. To fearlessly reach out in compassion to those who seem to purposely make themselves hard to love.

I've seen lives changed in amazing ways when believers do this. One of the first such changes I saw took place in the life of a man I encountered while out witnessing many years ago with a group of believers in Lompoc, California. I'll never forget it. We had purposely gone to an area where a lot of people were strung out on drugs. As we were preaching and mingling with the people, one little woman in our group zeroed in on an unsavory-looking man who was obviously high on some illegal substance, and started talking to him about Jesus.

We found out later the man was the biggest drug dealer in the whole area. The woman with us wasn't more than about five feet tall. However, she wasn't a bit frightened of him. Even when he ordered her to leave him alone, she kept telling him that God loved him. She turned the other cheek when he rebuffed her, and kept trying to help him. Finally, after the man let her know in no uncertain terms that he was not interested in what she had to say, she told him that if he didn't make a change, he was going to get arrested.

"I've never been busted by the cops in my life and I'm not about to start now!" he said.

Under the Protective Umbrella of God

You can guess what happened. The next day, the police showed up and arrested him. In jail, he couldn't stop thinking about what she had been telling him. He remembered how she kept talking to him and reaching out to him even after he was so mean to her. (Unbelievers don't understand that kind of unselfish Love. It's beyond their ability to grasp. Yet when it's real and not counterfeit, they're drawn to it.)

Regretting that he hadn't listened when he had the chance, the man started shouting and throwing things around in his cell. "I want to go down there to the church where that bunch are preaching about Jesus," he yelled. "If somebody doesn't take me there, I'm going to tear up this whole jail!"

That morning, we had a 10 o'clock service scheduled. About ten minutes after it started, a black-and-white squad car pulled up and let the man out. He came to the meeting, received Jesus as The LORD of his life, and was baptized in the Holy Spirit. After the service, he asked us where we were going next. We told him we were headed for Florida to do the same thing there we'd been doing in California. "I want to go with you," he said. "I want to bust some heads for Jesus!"

As a brand-new believer, the first thing that man wanted to do was get involved with other people. The moment the Love of God was shed abroad in his heart, he wanted to share it. He wanted to find someone who was as hopeless as he'd been the previous day and tell them the same good news our friend had told him.

That particular incident took place in the early 1970s. We saw a lot of fearless young believers like her back then. That was an era when primarily teenagers and people in their twenties were fired up about Jesus. They were charging unafraid into sin-darkened places to tell people about Him.

LIVE FEAR FREE

It was the era of people like David Wilkerson.

A young pastor originally from Indiana, David went to New York in the 1960s to minister to teenagers in the street gangs. He loved them instead of being afraid of them, shared Jesus with them, and wound up winning the most infamous gang leader at the time, young Nicky Cruz, to The LORD. I once talked to a man who knew Nicky and his story very well. He told me about the time Nicky tried to stab David Wilkerson but found he couldn't touch him. "Nicky," the young pastor said, "if you cut me into a thousand pieces, every one of them would still say I love you."

In these last days before Jesus returns, we're going to hear more such testimonies. Increasing numbers of fired-up believers will be taking the good news about Jesus to dangerous people in dangerous places. When some of those believers show up in your church, don't be surprised if, instead of attending the ice cream social, they go out on the streets to share Jesus with the socially unacceptable. Don't scold them when they insist on going into dumps and dives to tell people about Him.

Even if God doesn't call you to go with them into those dumps and dives, encourage them. Pray for them. Cheer them on. Then do your part by showing compassion to the hard-to-love people that come across your own path.

No matter where you go, you're not going to escape having to deal with hard-to-love people. The world is full of them!

Sometimes it will seem like they purposely seek you out just to antagonize you. Someone you haven't heard from in ages might call you on the telephone just to chew you out about some remark you made twenty years ago. (That's actually happened to me.)

It's not easy to respond to such people by loving them and turning the other cheek. It requires us to say no to our flesh. But

Under the Protective Umbrella of God

when we do that, we're acting like Jesus. He said, "If any man will come after me, let him deny himself, and take up his cross, and follow me" (Matthew 16:24).

People sometimes say things like, "I guess this back pain I have is just my cross to bear." Or, "I guess these money problems I'm always having are just my cross to bear." But that's not what Jesus meant when He told us to take up our cross.

Pain and sickness aren't our cross. Financial lack isn't our cross. Jesus bore those things on *His* cross so we wouldn't have to bear them. The cross He called us to bear—the one thing we will always have in our lives until He returns to this earth—is selfish, unlovely people.

Some of those people are Christians, but they listen to the devil more than they listen to God, so they don't act very Christian. If something doesn't go their way, they throw a fit. As unpleasant as they may be, though, they still need someone to minister to them. Their burdens still need to be borne, often by someone else who knows how to pray and believe God. So, as followers of Jesus, that's what we do. We take up our cross by loving those who are hardest to love, knowing that even if we have to piggyback the whole bunch into heaven, it will be worth it to get them there.

Most likely though, the hardest-to-love people in your life will be unbelievers. Reaching out to them with the Love of Jesus can be especially uncomfortable. So much so, that sometimes, when they need that Love the most, you might be tempted to let fear stop you from doing for them what Compassion is moving you to do.

I remember one instance when Jerry Savelle found himself in such a situation when we were in a certain city preaching a series of meetings. We didn't have a service scheduled on Sunday

155

LIVE FEAR FREE

morning, so he had gone downtown to witness to people. While he was walking around, he saw a man fall down in the street and begin to have a hard seizure.

Although there were other people around, no one tried to help. They just stared at the man, afraid to do anything. But rather than being moved by fear, Jerry was moved by compassion. He jumped into the middle of the street, laid his hands on that man, and said to the devil, "Come out of him, in the Name of Jesus!"

Jerry told me later he had plenty of room to work that day because everyone else backed away from him. They stopped staring at the man having the seizure and started staring at Jerry as if to say, *What in the world are you doing?*

Jerry, however, wasn't focused on what people were thinking about him. That's not the yardstick by which he was measuring. The yardstick he was using was the Love of God, so He did for that man what Love Himself would do. As a result, the man was delivered from the seizure and received Jesus as his LORD and Savior right there in the street.

"But Brother Copeland, I don't travel around like you ministers do. I don't have a lot of time to walk around downtown looking for people who need Jesus' Love."

Then love people wherever you happen to be. If you're a businessperson, for example, minister the Love of Jesus to the people with whom you do business. Instead of just looking out for your own interests, look out for the other fellow's as well. That's like a sign and a wonder to unbelievers.

It will cause them to wonder about you just as it caused the unsaved owner of a radio station to wonder about a friend of mine when they were making a business deal. My friend wanted to buy the man's station and, knowing the owner was Jewish, as they were

Under the Protective Umbrella of God

negotiating a price, my friend said, "According to The WORD of God, whoever BLESSES the seed of Abraham will be BLESSED. So, I am going to see to it that you get the best end of this deal."

Most people would consider my friend foolish. They'd think he was setting himself up to be taken advantage of. But he wasn't. He was setting himself up to succeed because Love never fails.

I've learned that if I'm doing what God said, no one can take advantage of me. No one can rob me. Someone may get some of my stuff, but I'll give it to them faster than they can walk off with it. I'll get back more than they stole, because Jesus said, "Give, and it will be given to you: good measure, pressed down, shaken together, and running over will be put into your bosom" (Luke 6:38, *New King James Version).*

This is how we, as believers, are supposed to operate, but the Jewish owner of the radio station my friend was buying didn't understand it. He said, "Why would you promise to give me the best end of the deal? No one has ever taken that attitude toward me in a business transaction."

My friend became a very strong Christian witness to that Jewish businessman. And the deal turned out to be the best one my friend ever made. The man became determined to help him every way he could, and eventually they wound up in the radio business together—preaching the gospel!

BEAUTIFUL FEET

When you are motivated by Love and not selfishness and fear, you start looking for opportunities to get involved in the lives of other people. Unlike the world, you don't run from such involvement, you actually seek out people to BLESS. You become an intercessor, praying for God to bring across your path those who need Him, those who are hurting whom you can help.

157

LIVE FEAR FREE

One group of women from a church I've been associated with for many years started praying that way after they'd seemingly hit a brick wall trying to win people to Jesus in their neighborhood. For months, everywhere they went, their words seemed to just fall on deaf ears. Finally, the pastor's wife decided they should change their approach. "Instead of praying for success, let's pray for the people out there who need Jesus," she said. "Let's intercede for them in Love, and ask The LORD to lead us to them."

As they were praying, God gave the pastor's wife a vision. She saw an apartment door with a number on it and a street sign. Not knowing what would happen, she and another member of the prayer group located the street and found the apartment. When they knocked on the door, someone opened it and invited them in.

Once inside, they saw a sick woman lying in bed. "Praise God!" the sick woman shouted, "I saw you pray for me in a vision this morning and saw myself get healed." The pastor's wife laid hands on her, and out of the bed she came, instantly healed!

This is how lives are changed! You can pass out gospel tracts and organize all kinds of evangelistic campaigns. But you won't really see supernatural results until you're moved by compassion to act on The WORD to pray and lay hands on people to get them set free—not to just to build a bigger church.

Romans 10:15 says, "How beautiful are the feet of them that preach the gospel of peace, and bring glad tidings of good things!" That's not just a sweet Bible verse; it's a powerful spiritual truth. There's nothing more beautiful than the gospel of peace to people who have been hopelessly trapped in turmoil and fear.

They're like the American civilian I heard about who spent much of World War II locked up in a prisoner of war camp. During his time there, his captors starved him and beat him. They

Under the Protective Umbrella of God

stripped him of all hope and told him the United States had fallen and lost the war, and that he would never be rescued.

Then one day, he heard a roar. Looking up, he saw a sky full of B-29 bombers. Spotting the big blue and white stars painted underneath the wings, he realized the truth: His captors had lied to him! The next day, when a U.S. soldier—not a general, just an infantryman—kicked open the door to his cell, the once-hopeless prisoner fell to the ground and kissed the soldier's boots.

That's what freedom is like to a man who has been bound! It's why the feet of those who bring the good news are beautiful to those who've been locked up in sin. The devil has lied to them. He's told the drug addict he has to die of that addiction, that he can never be free—that there's no way out for him.

But then someone with the Love of God in his or her heart shows up. Some believer comes along who's not afraid of the ugliness of addiction. Someone like you looks at them not with condemnation but with compassion, tells them the good news about Jesus, and offers to pray for that sin-imprisoned person, even when he's throwing up all over the floor.

When you put your hand on his head and God delivers and makes him a new creation, he feels like kissing your feet.

Beautiful are the feet of those who carry the gospel of The LORD Jesus Christ.

That gospel is the only chance a dying man has, and *you* are a carrier of it.

Take it to everyone you can and share it with Love, unhindered by the fear of man.

Beautiful are *your* feet!

CHAPTER 9

SAFE IN THE ALMIGHTY ARMS OF LOVE

CHAPTER 9

Safe in the Almighty Arms of Love

Be strong and of a good courage, fear not, nor be afraid of them:
for The LORD thy God, he it is that doth go with thee;
he will not fail thee, nor forsake thee.
(Deuteronomy 31:6)

THE LORD SAID THIS TO me one time, and it changed my life: *The reason most people have trouble with fear is because they're trying to be their own God.*

That's not just true of unbelievers. It's true of Christians as well.

We would never intentionally try to be our own God, of course. We know better than that. Yet at times, we've all found ourselves in a seemingly dire situation and reacted as if the outcome totally depended on us. *How am I going to get out of this?* we've thought. *How am I going to come up with the money to meet this need? What am I going to do? WHAT AM I GOING TO DO?*

When you're thinking like that, you're looking only to yourself for answers. You're trying to figure out on your own how you're going to solve a problem you don't have the power to solve. Instead of looking *to* God, you're acting as if you *are* God.

LIVE FEAR FREE

That opens the door to fear and ultimately to failure.

Why?

Because you're not qualified to be God.

You do, however, have a Blood Covenant with the One who is—your all-powerful, omniscient, heavenly Father! He is your Covenant God. He is more than able to solve any problem, meet your every need, and protect you from any threat. His Love for you is fierce, vast and everlasting, and He has said to you: "Be strong and of a good courage, fear not, nor be afraid...for The LORD thy God, he it is that doth go with thee; he will not fail thee, nor forsake thee" (Deuteronomy 31:6).

I like the way the last part of that verse reads where it's quoted in the New Testament book of Hebrews:

[God] Himself has said, I will not in any way fail you nor give you up nor leave you without support. [I will] not, [I will] not, [I will] not in any degree leave you helpless *nor* forsake nor let [you] down (relax My hold on you)! [Assuredly not!] (Hebrews 13:5, *Amplified Bible, Classic Edition).*

In other words, as a believer, you're not on your own—ever, in any situation. You don't have to know all the answers to all the questions that confront you. You don't have to possess all the power and financial resources to triumph over all the troubles that arise. You just have to remember that the One who does have all those things is always with you and backing you all the way.

If you remember that, when seemingly insoluble problems arise, you won't be shaken. When the devil starts pressuring you and asking you what you're going to do, you can just say, "I don't know yet. I'm not God. But He is with me, and He can handle anything. So, I'm just going to be still and know that He is God, have faith in Him, and do whatever He says."

Especially in these last days before Jesus returns, it's wonderful not to have to figure things out on your own. It's marvelous to be able to just let God be God in your life. He's the only One with the wisdom and ability to navigate these perilous times. Human wisdom won't get the job done. That's why Jesus said, at the end of the age, nations will be "in bewilderment and perplexity [without resources, left wanting, embarrassed, in doubt, not knowing which way to turn]" (Luke 21:25, *Amplified Bible, Classic Edition).*

For people who don't know The LORD, the earth is going to become increasingly scary. But not for believers. We don't have to be afraid of anything because when human wisdom fails, unlike the world, we *do* know where to turn. We can look to our God who knows everything. We can be strong and of good courage not only because is He in us and with us always, but because "we have known and believed the Love that He hath to us" (1 John 4:16).

We've already seen that walking in perfected Love casts out fear. But it's also important for us to realize that Love doesn't start with us. It starts with God who's in us. The reason we can trust Him enough to do whatever He says is because we're confident in His Love for us. That confidence enables us to love others and, in so doing, brings His Love to completion and accomplishes what God intended in us.

Look again at what 1 John 4 says about this:

Herein is Love, not that we loved God, but that he loved us, and sent his Son to be the propitiation for our sins. Beloved, if God so loved us, we ought also to love one another.... If we love one another, God dwelleth in us, and

LIVE FEAR FREE

his Love is perfected in us…. And we have known and believed the Love that God hath to us…. There is no fear in Love; but perfect Love casteth out fear: because fear hath torment. He that feareth is not made perfect in Love. We love him, because he first loved us (verses 10-12, 16-19).

Notice those verses don't say God's Love is *perfected* in us simply because we've known it. If that's all it took, we'd all be walking in perfected Love because, as believers, we've all known God's Love.

You knew His Love the instant you were born again. It was His Love that re-created your spirit. It was His Love that brought you out from under the authority of darkness and translated you into the kingdom of God's dear Son. If you went to church as a child, the first song you probably learned was *Jesus Loves Me, This I Know.*

Knowing God's Love, though, is just half the equation. Verse 16 says, "We have known *and believed*" His Love. The believing part is what tends to trip us up. So, if we've done everything we know to do and we're still struggling with fear, the question we need to ask ourselves is not do we know God's Love, but do we have faith in it? Do we believe it?

Many Christians don't.

You can tell by how they talk. They say things like, "I just don't feel like God loves me. I'm doing the best I can to trust Him with everything I'm going through, but I feel so spiritually dry. Sometimes I feel like God just doesn't care about me. I don't feel very loved at all."

What's the problem? They're making the same mistake we identified earlier when we talked about walking in Love toward others. They're focusing on their feelings. The Bible doesn't say that we have known and *felt* the Love that God hath to us. It says we have known and *believed* it.

To believe means to have faith, and faith doesn't come from looking at our feelings. It comes from hearing The WORD of God.

A BLOOD COVENANT OF LOVE

Feelings change but God's WORD never changes. So by focusing on what The WORD says, we can have faith in God's Love no matter how we might be feeling. If we're feeling spiritually dry, we can turn to scriptures like those in 1 John 4. We can meditate on them and fellowship with the Holy Spirit over them until the revelation of just how much God loves us rises up in our hearts.

Look at verse 9, for instance. It says, "In this was manifested the Love of God toward us, because that God sent his only begotten Son into the world, that we might live through him." There's enough revelation in just that one verse to cause your faith level to rise sky-high.

Think about it. Why would Almighty God send His dearly beloved Son from heaven to this sin-corrupted earth? Why would Jesus come down from glory to live in this doubt-filled, hate-infested, stealing, killing world that, compared to heaven, is a pigsty of a place? Why would a member of the Godhead limit Himself by taking on human flesh?

Think about how much Jesus must love us to have been willing to make such a sacrifice!

When He came to earth to be our Savior, He laid aside all His divine privileges and power. "He became like men and was born a human being" (Philippians 2:7, *Amplified Bible, Classic Edition*). He had to start out as a baby, just as we do, and grow up

LIVE FEAR FREE

both physically and spiritually. He had to learn and grow in The WORD. He had to find out from the Scriptures who He was and live in perfect obedience to God.

Then, He had to die on the Cross and go to hell in our place. Think about the risk He took! No one had ever gotten out of hell before. But Jesus went there and believed God to raise Him up. And on the third day, He came out of that pit to become the first resurrected, glorified Man!

That's how much Jesus loves us! He didn't just become a Man for the thirty-three years He was on earth. He became a Man forever. He is still a Man today. His glorified physical body still bears the marks of His Crucifixion. He still has the holes in His hands and His side, and the scars on His head.

Those are Covenant scars. They're eternal reminders of the unmeasurable, unfailing, everlasting Love that your heavenly Father and The LORD Jesus Christ have for you. They're proof that the New Covenant is an everlasting Blood Covenant of Love. A Covenant from which, as far as God is concerned, there is no retreat and about which there is no debate.

Through His Covenant, God said, "I love you," and there's nothing you can do to change that. You can choose to believe it or not, but either way, He will still love you because the Covenant has been made.

God would love you all the way to hell if you chose to go there. He loves you no matter how bad you've been or what a sorry loser you might think you are. He loved the Apostle Paul who, by his own admission, was the chief of all sinners. Paul participated in the killing of Christians before he was born again. Yet God made an apostle out of him!

Hard to imagine? Yes, but that's how powerful God's Love is.

Safe in the Almighty Arms of Love

It can do more for you than you can ask or think. But for it to do so, you must have faith in it. You must keep believing the Love God has for you regardless of what your emotions might be telling you. You must believe that He loves you when you *feel* like He does...and when you don't.

Really, it's when you aren't feeling very loved that you most need to believe it. It's when you're feeling spiritually dry that the devil will try to use your emotions to manipulate you. But you can shut his operations down fast by simply giving voice to your faith instead of your feelings.

You can start praising The LORD and saying, "How I feel doesn't change anything. The WORD of God hasn't changed, and it says that my God loves me! He loves me so much that Jesus left His place of glory, put on a flesh body, suffered, died, went to hell and was raised from the dead *for me*. He is my LORD and Savior, and He said, 'I will never leave you, nor forsake you!'"

If you'll start declaring The WORD instead of just giving in to your feelings and the lies of the devil, your spiritually dry emotions will be awakened. Before long, you'll be dancing around and full of joy, celebrating your status as a dearly beloved child of God.

You won't be worrying about the perils in this world and wondering if God cares enough to protect you from them. On the contrary! In the light of all Jesus did to become your Savior, you'll think, *If Jesus loves me that much, I know He'll protect me. Whatever happens in this world, He will take care of me.*

LIVE FEAR FREE

STICK WITH GOD'S PLAN AND YOU WON'T NEED A WHALE

"But Brother Copeland," someone might say, "can I really be as sure of God's protection as I am of His Love? After all, He loves everyone, but He obviously doesn't protect everyone."

He would if they'd let Him. Many people, however, won't. As a result, even though God loves them, He can't do much for them.

God has trouble protecting unbelievers, for example, because they haven't entered into Covenant relationship with Him. They haven't given Him the legal right to intervene in their lives.

He has trouble protecting believers at times because, although they're in Covenant relationship with Him, they won't listen to Him. They won't cooperate with Him and do what He says.

It happens all too often. God will speak to a believer and say something as simple as, *Don't go to that party tonight.* But they'll ignore Him. They'll go to the party and wind up getting hurt. He'll speak to another believer and tell them to go a certain place and do something for Him, but they'll choose not to do it. They'll come up with their own idea and get into trouble by being in the wrong place at the wrong time.

If you've ever read about Jonah in the Bible, you'll remember that's what happened to him. God told him to go to Nineveh and preach, and he decided he'd rather not. He boarded a ship headed for somewhere else instead, got caught in a violent storm, and was thrown overboard by the crew (Jonah 1:14-15).

It wasn't God's fault Jonah wound up in the sea. God didn't put him there. Jonah put himself there. But here's the good news: God is so merciful and mighty that even then, He was able to save Jonah's life. He sent a whale to swallow him, and in the belly of the whale, Jonah repented. He put himself back under God's

Safe in the Almighty Arms of Love

protection, and the whale "vomited out Jonah upon the dry land" (Jonah 2:10).

That was undoubtedly an unpleasant experience. But getting coughed up on the shore alive is certainly better than being washed up on the shore dead. And if it hadn't been for the whale, Jonah would have drowned. So, the whale wasn't a punishment. It was a manifestation of God's mercy.

I know about that kind of mercy. God had to send a whale for me when I was twenty-seven years old. I put myself and my family in the wrong place at the wrong time for much the same reason Jonah did—because I decided to not obey God. He told me to move to Tulsa, Oklahoma, and enroll as a student at Oral Roberts University and, for three years, I ignored what He said. Afraid that as a full-time student I wouldn't be able to financially support my family, I told Gloria, "If we go up there to that university, we'll starve."

"Kenneth, we're starving now," she said. "We might as well starve in the will of God as out of the will of God."

I couldn't really argue with that, but fear continued to hold me back. At the time, I'd been born again for several years but I was still a scriptural illiterate. Unlike Gloria, I hadn't spent any time in The WORD, so I didn't yet have much of a revelation of God's Love. I hadn't developed enough faith in it to trust He would help me in Tulsa and not fail me.

So, I came up with another plan. Instead of going to Tulsa and attending ORU, I accepted a position at a church in Houston. Although we hadn't moved there yet, one night I was driving my family from Houston to Arkansas when, just outside of Marshall, Texas, someone pulled out from a side road directly in front of us. With no time to stop, our car T-boned theirs, then slammed into the ditch beside the road.

LIVE FEAR FREE

The impact was horrific, and because there were no seat belt laws or children's car seats back then, in the natural, there was little to protect us.

Gloria (who had the flu at the time) hit the metal dashboard with such force that her head left a half-moon-shaped dent in it. Our son, John, who was less than a year old and had been asleep on a blanket between Gloria and me, was thrown under the front seat, suffered a broken arm, and had four ribs torn loose from his spine. Our daughter, Kellie, who was in the back seat, got thrown around but didn't break any bones. And though I should have been crushed and impaled on the steering column, I came out with no serious injuries.

The devil had intended to kill us all. Our car was demolished. It was only by the grace of God any of us survived.

That night, like Jonah in the whale, I wasn't arguing with God anymore. I was repenting for not doing what He said. As I sat in the hospital rocking little bandaged-up John, looking at Kellie piled up there in the bed, and Gloria with her face all bruised, I prayed, "Oh, LORD, forgive me."

After I'd been praying for a few minutes, two men slipped into the room and joined me. I realized they were there when I saw their bare feet walk up behind my rocking chair. I thought, *I don't know anybody in this town. Who could these people be?* Then they started praying in tongues, and I decided I didn't care. I thought, *Glory to God, whoever they are, let them pray!*

After a few moments, one of them leaned over close to me and asked, "Are you Pentecostal?"

"Yes, I am," I replied.

"This fellow here is a Church of Christ brother," the man said, pointing to his friend. "I won him to The LORD yesterday and

Safe in the Almighty Arms of Love

got him baptized in the Holy Spirit. I'm here in the hospital because I had a wreck in my truck and my company put me in here. There's not a thing wrong with me, but on account of the insurance I had to stay a couple of days. We would have been down here to pray earlier, but the nurse told us she would kick us out of the hospital. So, we hid behind the water cooler until she left."

As they prayed, the power of God came on me and into that room. Gloria went to sleep and was healed of the flu. Kellie went to sleep and was healed. John went to sleep on my chest and was healed. The two men left after they prayed, but I sat there another forty-five minutes or so, rocking John, praying in the Holy Spirit, and praising The LORD.

I called my parents, and the next morning they came to get us. As we were riding along, my dad asked me what Gloria and I were going to be doing the next week. I told him I didn't know. He reminded me that he and my mother were partners with Oral Roberts' ministry. "You know, they have partner meetings at ORU from time to time," he said, "and we got our invitations a few days ago. But they sent us four this time instead of two. Would you and Gloria like to go with us?"

"Yes, yes, yes!" I exclaimed.

You see, God was working the whole time. And when I got back under His umbrella of protection, things started working for me instead of against me. When I stopped trying to be my own God and just started listening to and doing what He said, I really started to see what He can do!

When the time came for me to register for school and I didn't have money to pay my tuition, instead of trying to come up with a solution myself, I went to The LORD to get the answer. "I'm going to pray all night if that's what it takes," I told Gloria.

LIVE FEAR FREE

After praying in the spirit for a while, since I hadn't yet heard anything from Him, I thought, *Maybe if I just get quiet here for a while, God will speak to me.* Sure enough, He did. He didn't speak to me in an audible voice, but He spoke inside me so loudly that even my hair heard it!

It's about time! He said. *I haven't been able to get a word in edgewise. Get up on your feet. I called you here, and I'll take care of you here! This school can't make a minister out of you. I've already made a minister out of you. All they can do is train you. Your ministry doesn't start after you get out of school. It starts now!*

After He finished speaking to me, I went back in where Gloria was. "What happened to praying all night?" she asked. "I got my direction," I said.

The next day, I went to the registrar's office to pay the first quarter of my tuition. I still didn't have any money, but after what I'd heard from God there was no way I was going back home. So, not knowing what else to do, I decided to call my dad.

I asked the registrar, Mrs. Campbell, as she hammered away on the typewriter typing up my bill, "Is it OK if I make a collect call?"

"Yes," she said, still hammering away. "Dial 9."

After my dad and I exchanged hellos and I told him where I was, he said, "Kenneth, Eddie Matthews stopped by with a check and said it's for your ministry." *What?* Eddie Matthews was in the construction business, and I hardly knew him! Although he had met my dad years before through the Full Gospel Business Men's Fellowship, he had no idea where I was on the planet.

"How much is the check?" I asked.

It was exactly the amount I needed to pay my first quarter's tuition.

174

Safe in the Almighty Arms of Love

After finishing up in the registrar's office, as I was leaving the Learning Resources Center, The LORD stopped me.

Go up to the sixth floor, He said.

"I can't go up there. That's the Vatican!" I told Him. I called it the Vatican because it was the executive floor. Off-limits to students, it was where Brother Roberts', Dean Messick's and Ron Smith's offices were. *They work for Me,* The LORD said.

I got in the elevator, but I still couldn't make myself press the button for the sixth floor. So instead, I pressed five and stepped out into what turned out to be where the future library would eventually be. *I said the sixth floor!* The LORD repeated.

Back in the elevator, I forced myself to press six and when the doors opened, I walked up to the first person I saw. As I found out later, she was Ruth Rooks, Brother Roberts' executive assistant. Once again, I didn't know what to do, so I just said, "I'm Kenneth Copeland. I'm thirty years old and I'm a student here. I'm a commercially rated pilot. I understand you use aircraft here, and I can use all the help I can get."

Mrs. Rooks replied, "Tell Dean Messick." I said the same thing to him, and he just said, *"Hmph."* So, I turned around to leave…and found myself facing Oral Roberts. He had walked up behind me while I was talking.

He introduced himself and after I stuttered around for a few seconds he said, "I understand you're a commercially rated pilot. Can you handle our airplane?"

I told him yes, and he continued. "Two weeks ago, I started to hire a co-pilot, and The LORD said, *No, I have a student coming who's supposed to have the job.* You're my man."

LIVE FEAR FREE

FREE FROM THE CURSE, AND UNDER THE BLOOD

God could have done all those things for me three years earlier. He could have not only provided for me financially but kept me from having that car wreck. That was certainly His will. I just fouled things up. Even so, however, He preserved me and my family, saved our lives, and got us back on track.

Saving us is what Jesus does! It's why He came to earth—to be our Savior.

What did He come to save us from?

Anything and everything we need to be saved from—spirit, soul and body, financially and socially.

What's more, our Savior is also our Big Brother. We have the same heavenly Father. When we mess up, Big Brother steps in and makes it all right for us (1 John 2). He says, "Father, I'll fix this," and the Father says, "All right, You go ahead and fix it for them, Jesus."

Back in 1966, I wasn't as clear about that as I am now. Sitting there next to my dad in the front seat as we drove back to Fort Worth after the wreck, I just kept thinking, *Oh, LORD, I've made such a mess of things.*

At times like that, the devil starts working on you. He tells you that you don't deserve to have Jesus fix the mess you made. He tries to get you into fear by telling you that you're not worthy of God's help. He'll tell you that because you didn't do things exactly right, you'll just have to suffer the consequences of the curse that comes with breaking God's law.

The devil says those kinds of things to all of us as believers. But remember, he is a liar. The truth is, we are worthy! Jesus'

176

Safe in the Almighty Arms of Love

blood has made us worthy, and He is our Redeemer. As Galatians 3:13-14 says:

> Christ hath redeemed us from the curse of the law, being made a curse for us: for it is written, Cursed is every one that hangeth on a tree: that THE BLESSING of Abraham might come on the Gentiles through Jesus Christ; that we might receive the promise of the Spirit through faith.

Those verses ought to be part of your daily vocabulary. You ought to be like a loaded gun with a hair trigger, so that when the devil tries to scare you by threatening you with some aspect of the curse, you can fire right back at him and say, "No, the curse will not come into my house! I am redeemed from it. I'm walking in THE BLESSING. I'm BLESSED coming in and going out. I'm BLESSED with health. I'm BLESSED financially. I'm BLESSED with protection from all evil! My God loves me. I have favorite-child status. I am the redeemed of The LORD, and I stand on the redemptive blood that was shed for me."

When you stand on the blood of Jesus, you're standing on the ultimate expression of God's Love! You're invoking His full Covenant protection. By using your words of faith to apply "the Blood of the everlasting Covenant" (Hebrews 13:20), you're bringing the very life and power of God on the scene to do for you everything He promised in the Bible—including protect you from every manifestation of the curse.

You can see an example of how effective such protection can be in the book of Exodus. There, God used blood to protect the Israelites from the plague that struck Egypt and killed all the firstborn in the land. Before the plague hit, He commanded every Israelite family to sacrifice a lamb. He instructed them to put its blood over and upon the doorposts of their homes. And they were to stay inside all night and not go out.

LIVE FEAR FREE

"The blood shall be to you for a token upon the houses where ye are: and when I see the blood, I will pass over you, and the plague shall not be upon you to destroy you," He said (Exodus 12:13).

Imagine what that night must have been like for the Israelites! Imagine yourself in their place:

You've put the blood on the doorpost, and though outside darkness has fallen, you're sitting inside your house where it's light and safe. Suddenly you start hearing screams in the distance. "My baby is dead! My brother is dead!" You hear the lowing of cattle as the firstborn of the Egyptians' livestock are struck by the plague and start to die.

Outside, the sounds of tragedy and death are filling the air. But in your house, as in all the other houses in your neighborhood where the blood has been applied, no one is sick. No one is dying. All is well.

If God could provide that kind of protection for the Israelites with the blood of a little innocent animal, how much more can the precious, sinless blood of Jesus protect us as believers?

Hebrews 12:24 says Jesus' blood "speaks better things." His blood has a voice! It's a voice God always hears. It's the fiercely protective voice of Covenant Love.

When I think of that Love, I'm reminded of how fiercely protective my mother was of me when I was growing up. She loved me so much she would have fought a cage full of bobcats to protect me. If anyone or anything threatened to hurt me, her little Cherokee Indian eyes would start flashing. Suddenly, it wasn't just Momma you were seeing, it was Momma's love.

That protective kind of Love is what the blood of Jesus brings forth from God. When the Blood speaks, it's Love saying, "Be

178

Safe in the Almighty Arms of Love

strong and of a good courage, fear not, nor be afraid…for The LORD thy God, he it is that doth go with thee; he will not fail thee, nor forsake thee." (Deuteronomy 31:6). It's the Blood of the everlasting Covenant saying, "I will not fail thee, nor forsake thee. I love you and I'll protect you. I'll fight your fight for you. I'll provide for you. Go on and do what I told you to do. Don't be afraid, because Love is right here."

As God sees it, when anyone or anything threatens you, they're threatening Him. That's why in Acts 9, Jesus said to Saul when he was breathing out threatenings and slaughter against the Church, "Why are you persecuting Me?" He didn't say, "Why are you persecuting the Church?" or "Why are you persecuting Christians?" He took it personally.

In Matthew 25:40, Jesus said, "Inasmuch as ye have done it unto one of the least of these my brethren, ye have done it unto me." So, anything the devil does to you, he's doing to Jesus. Anytime he attacks you or your family in some way, he's attacking Love Himself, and as long as you stay in faith under the blood, Love Himself will defend and protect you.

Believing God loves you that much will wash fear right out of you!

Crises in the world that used to scare you will come and go, and you won't even know they happened. You'll quit listening to what's being said about them on television because there's no use in bothering with it. After all, you have a Blood Covenant of protection. You don't have to join in on a recession. You don't have to fall prey to the latest plague. You don't have to be terrified by terrorism. You can listen to God, do what He says, and keep on rejoicing—safe and BLESSED in the Almighty arms of Love.

CHAPTER 10

AS ASHES UNDER YOUR FEET

CHAPTER 10

As Ashes Under Your Feet

*"But to you who fear My name the Sun of Righteousness
shall arise with healing in His wings; and you shall go out
and grow fat like stall-fed calves. You shall trample the wicked,
for they shall be ashes under the soles of your feet on the day
that I do this," says The LORD of hosts.
(Malachi 4:2–3, New King James Version)*

Do you know what the devil sees when he looks at fear-free, faith-and-Love-filled believers who are on fire for Jesus?

He sees spiritual terrorists!

He sees Christians he can no longer control with his threats and fearmongering, and against whom he has no defense. He sees believers who, instead of cowering under his attacks, now leave him cowering under theirs. He sees believers who know the victory that's theirs in Christ and cannot be stopped from doing the works of Jesus. He is well aware they know who they are in Jesus and will trample him and his works as ashes under the soles of their feet.

That's the kind of believer every one of us was born again to be!

LIVE FEAR FREE

It's the kind of believer I saw my mother become during her lifetime. She was the first up-close example I ever saw of someone who knew how to terrify the devil. She dealt with him with such bold ferocity, particularly when she was praying for someone, that if you saw her do it, you'd assumed she had always been totally fearless. But she hadn't.

Although from the time she was a little girl, my mother had always loved The LORD and loved to pray, for many years she was an extremely fearful person.

I don't know for sure, but I suspect fear gained a foothold in her life through an incident that happened to her in high school. While on the basketball court, her appendix burst, and she nearly died. She was so far gone by the time they got her to the hospital, the doctor who operated on her didn't even bother to sew up the incision. He just closed it up with cadaver clamps because he fully expected her to die.

When he delivered the news to her parents, her father essentially told him, "If she dies, you die." So, the doctor went back in and stitched her up. Since he still didn't expect her to survive, he didn't bother to put everything back like he should have. As a result, the lower part of her body was left so messed up that the doctor told her she would only live, at most, for ten more years, and that she could never have children.

When she didn't die after the first ten years, the doctors repeated the prognosis. When she lived another ten years, the prognosis was repeated. Decade after decade, she was told she wouldn't live more than ten additional years. So, the threat of death continually hung over her.

By the time she married, she was so afraid that the first time my dad made plans to travel on an airliner, she panicked. She tried to talk him into driving or taking a train, but he explained that would take too long and, despite her objections, boarded a DC-3 to fly from Abilene, Texas, to California to see his parents. After the plane took off, my mother went home and went to bed for three days. "We'll never see him again," she said.

Although she wasn't that afraid in every area, for years some things frightened her so much they just about made her sick. But in the early 1960s, around the time Gloria and I were born again, she changed. She went to a week-long prayer camp and while she was there, the spirit of fear that had dominated her got cast out. It completely lost its power over her.

From that point on, she had absolutely no fear. She would get in an airplane and fly anywhere she wanted to go. She would preach The WORD, pray for people, and when demon spirits manifested, she'd laugh in their faces and cast them out. One night I overheard two Baptist preachers talking about it as they were leaving one of her prayer meetings. "Didn't that beat all you've ever seen?" one of them said. "It sure did!" replied the other. "I believe that's the first time in my entire life I ever felt sorry for the devil."

Once free from fear, my mother made the devil sorry for the rest of her life. She launched an attack against his works and never let up. She terrorized him until the day she went to heaven and, as a result, she BLESSED and changed countless lives.

Now The LORD is raising up an entire spiritual army of such believers. He's teaching us all how to live free from fear in these last days, not just because it's a more enjoyable way to live, but because the hour is late. We can't afford to waste time anymore, letting the devil use fear to control us. We have a lot to do before Jesus returns and only a short time left in which to do it.

LIVE FEAR FREE

When I say *a short time,* I really mean short!

All the way back in 2001, after the terror attack on September 11, The LORD told me we had entered the very last of the last days. He said we had moved out of what Jesus called "the beginning of sorrows" (Matthew 24:8) into the preamble to the Tribulation.

Thankfully, the preamble is all we, as believers, will experience. Before the Tribulation actually begins, we'll be out of here because that's when the wrath of God will come on the world, and as believers we're not appointed to that (1 Thessalonians 5:9). We're not objects of God's wrath, we are children of His Love. So, we'll be caught up to be with Him before the Tribulation starts.

> For The LORD himself shall descend from heaven with a shout, with the voice of the archangel, and with the trump of God: and the dead in Christ shall rise first: Then we which are alive and remain shall be caught up together with them in the clouds, to meet The LORD in the air: and so shall we ever be with The LORD (1 Thessalonians 4:16–17).

Before we're caught up to be with The LORD, however, we have a job to do. A big job. The LORD spoke to me about it in 2001 when He told me where we were on His timeline. In a voice so loud on the inside of me I heard it with every fiber of my being, He said, *Five billion people on the earth are headed for hell. That is an unacceptable casualty rate. I am not going to end this thing with that kind of failure. Not on My watch!*

In 2001, there were about six billion people on earth of which only one billion were Christians. Currently, earth's population is about 8.1 billion, of which an estimated 2.6 billion are Christians. So, although percentagewise we've made progress, what Jesus said to me still applies.

As Ashes Under Your Feet

There are still five billion people on earth headed for hell.

That is still an unacceptable casualty rate.

Jesus is not ending this thing with that kind of failure.

This is why we must declare war on fear and refuse to let the devil use it to control us. Someone has to go after those five billion souls. Someone has to get the gospel to them and love them into the kingdom of God. And we're the ones who are going to do it!

Unhindered by fear of the devil, fear of danger, financial fears, and the fear of man, we're going to go after the precious souls in our neighborhoods and communities. We're going to go after them in our nation. We're going to partner together and go after them in Asia, Africa, South America, the Middle East, Russia and Europe. We're going after them with The WORD and the Love of God wherever they are, all over the world.

We truly are about to become the devil's worst nightmare. An absolutely fearless troop of believers that he can't intimidate or frighten, we're going to snatch billions of souls out of the very jaws of hell, bring them over into the glory of God, and trample the devil as ashes under our feet.

I'M NOT RUNNING ANYMORE

"You better be careful talking like that, Brother Copeland," someone might say. "The devil is likely to hear you and come after you."

I want him to hear me! I'm not afraid of him and you shouldn't be either. Fear is his only weapon. As we've seen time and again, when you pull the plug on fear, you pull the plug on his power. He has nothing left. Unless He can draw you off through sin and selfishness into fear, he can't touch you.

LIVE FEAR FREE

He might puff himself up and threaten you, but apart from fear, the devil is about as dangerous as an eight-year-old knocking on your door wearing a spooky costume on Halloween. Would you be scared to see that little guy in the spooky suit standing on your porch? Would you worry that he might come after you? No, you might if you were four years old, but you're not. You're a grown-up. You know better.

The same holds true spiritually. Part of growing up in The LORD is learning better than to be afraid of the devil. It's learning to react to him like Smith Wigglesworth did. A great apostle of faith who preached during the early 1900s, he was such a threat to hell that satan himself showed up in his bedroom one night to threaten him. When Smith Wigglesworth woke up and saw him standing there, however, he didn't even bother to get out of bed. He just said, "Oh, it's only you" and went back to sleep.

I'll admit, the first time I encountered a demon spirit, because I was still very young in The LORD, I did not respond with that kind of confidence. Instead, when it spoke to me, the thing scared me silly. I'll never forget it. I had gone with a preacher friend to pray for a woman in the hospital. As I stood at the foot of the bed, she rolled her eyes, fixed them on me, and said in a bone-chilling voice, "Sit, boy! Sit! Sit!"

She couldn't have weighed more than seventy-five pounds, and back then I weighed over 240. But I ran from her, nevertheless. I bolted from her bedside and when I got out in the hall, my knees shaking, I thought, *Wait a minute, a seventy-five-pound woman has just run me out of the room, and I don't even know who she is.*

I didn't understand it. I wouldn't have been a bit intimidated if some big brute of a man had threatened me. In the natural, I had fought my way in and out of many such situations. But

188

when that demon tried to put the spirit of fear on me, I didn't know how to deal with it.

Right then and there, I made up my mind that I would never run from a demon again. I told The LORD, "I don't know much about what happened here, but I do know a born-again man doesn't have any business running away from someone who only weighs about seventy-five pounds. So You'll either have to teach me about this, or I'm going to get my block knocked off because, in the Name of Jesus, I declare it now: I am not running anymore!"

To learn what to do instead, I began studying the Gospel accounts of Jesus dealing with demon spirits. I read about how He ministered deliverance to people during His earthly ministry, and envisioned myself ministering deliverance just as He did. I meditated on that and thought about it until I had no fear at all of the devil, demons or evil spirits of any kind.

In the years that have passed since then, by the authority of Jesus' Name, the LORD has used me to get people delivered from all kinds of demon spirits in all kinds of places. I've cast demons out of people in locked and barred psychiatric wards, in homes or wherever I happened to encounter them. One woman I ministered to had been out of her mind for eighteen years. When she saw me, she screamed, "I know who you are, and you're afraid of anything that isn't flesh and blood!"

It was a demon spirit speaking through her, of course, just as it was a demon spirit that spoke to me through that little seventy-five-pound woman in the hospital years earlier. But this time, I didn't run. I stood my ground and calmly said, "No, ma'am. He that's within me is greater than he that's in the world. I have no fear of man nor beast, nor demons nor sin." Then I cast the devil out of that dear woman and got her delivered.

LIVE FEAR FREE

You can do the same thing when the devil shows up in your life. It doesn't matter how he manifests himself or how he tries to threaten you—whether it's through a demon-possessed person, a dangerous situation, or by showing up personally like he did in Smith Wigglesworth's bedroom. You don't ever have to run from him in fear.

Instead, you can turn the tables on him. You can do what James 4:7 says: Submit yourself to God, resist the devil, and he will flee from you. The Greek word translated *flee* in that verse means "to flee as if in terror."

The devil has no other choice but to run when you stand against him by faith in God's WORD, the Name of Jesus, and the blood of the New Covenant. You have the power of Almighty God backing you. Fleeing from you in terror is the devil's only option. He has no other choice.

THE SOLDIER'S PSALM

When it comes to standing in faith against the devil and his threats, one of the best passages of Scripture you can plant your feet on is Psalm 91. It's known as "The Soldier's Psalm." But it's not just for soldiers who are fighting in the natural for their country. It's for every one of us who have committed our lives to Jesus and become soldiers in the army of The LORD.

Especially in these dangerous last days, Psalm 91 ought to be to us, as believers, what General Orders are to those in the military. As I learned during my stint in the U.S. Army, General Orders are foundational. One of the first things every new recruit must do during boot camp is learn them well enough to recite them by heart, because they're vital to operational success and safety.

Psalm 91 is vital for us for the same reasons. Obeying its

As Ashes Under Your Feet

instructions will keep us under the umbrella of God's protection. Knowing and believing its promises will equip us to face any peril successfully and without fear.

I know of an infantry commander in World War I who proved this. A man of faith, he required every one of the 300 men in his company to learn Psalm 91. Whether they believed it or not, they had to be able to recite it. When he said to one of his soldiers, "Verse 2!" they had to say, "Sir, yes, sir! I will say of The LORD, He is my refuge and my fortress: my God; in him will I trust."

Every one of the soldiers who served under that commander made it through the war. He didn't lose one man. They didn't even experience any injuries. During World War I, for an entire infantry company to go into combat for a significant length of time without suffering any casualties was unheard of. But the Psalm 91 company did it.

A friend who is a full colonel and field grade officer in the U.S. military has a similar testimony. A Psalm 91 soldier himself, he was assigned to lead a unit known to have had a very high casualty rate. Before going into combat, he contacted me and asked me to lay hands on him.

We agreed together in faith on the promises in Psalm 91. I also ministered to him from Numbers 32:21-22, which says the soldier that goes to war armed before The LORD will return guiltless before God and the nation. Then I prayed over him.

Before he left the country to begin his tour of duty, he promised to give me a full report as soon as he returned. I didn't expect him to deliver it the moment his plane landed in the U.S. and his foot hit the tarmac, but he did. He called me at about 2:30 in the morning and, when I answered the phone, he was shouting.

LIVE FEAR FREE

"Praise God, Brother Kenneth! It worked! It worked!" he said. "Every man in my outfit learned the 91st Psalm. We stood on it. We believed it. We memorized it. We talked it. And not one of our men was killed. Not one! We didn't even have any serious casualties [injuries]. A few guys got hurt but they got healed."

That kind of supernatural protection is available to every one of us as believers. And whether we're on the battlefield or just going about our daily lives, we need to know how to walk in it. So, let's finish our study of fear-free living by spending some time in Psalm 91. Let's go through it verse by verse and get it down inside us more firmly than ever.

One thing I want to point out to you before we begin is this psalm's unusual grammatical structure. It indicates that some verses are spoken by one person and other verses are spoken by someone else. That's because there are three different individuals involved.

I'll point out who the other two are as we go along, but the first person who speaks is the psalmist himself. He begins the psalm by saying:

> He that dwelleth in the secret place of the most High shall abide under the shadow of the Almighty. I will say of The LORD, He is my refuge and my fortress: my God; in him will I trust (verses 1-2).

Notice, in just those two verses we learn two important things. First, we learn that when we are *dwelling* in the secret place of the Most High, we are abiding under His supernatural protection. To *dwell* in a place means to stay somewhere. To *abide* means to remain "stable and fixed" *(Amplified Bible, Classic Edition)*. In other words, we position ourselves in the place of God's protection not by just visiting Him occasionally and then going

192

As Ashes Under Your Feet

out and living like the world. We do it by dwelling, abiding and staying attached to Him.

The second thing we learn from these two verses is that we enter this secret place of God's protection with words of faith. We open our mouths and say of The LORD, "He is my Refuge and my Fortress, my God; on Him I lean and rely, and in Him I [confidently] trust!" *(Amplified Bible, Classic Edition).*

Those two things—staying attached to God and speaking words of faith—are our part of abiding in God's protection. So, once the psalmist has committed to do those two things, Someone else begins speaking in reply, declaring what Almighty God will do for us as secret-place dwellers. Who is this second Person? It's The LORD Jesus Christ!

Speaking to us as our Savior and the Mediator of our Covenant, He says:

Surely He [Almighty God] shall deliver you from the snare of the fowler and from the perilous pestilence. He shall cover you with His feathers, and under His wings you shall take refuge; His truth shall be your shield and buckler (verses 3-4, *New King James Version).*

The fact that the first word Jesus says there is "Surely" tells us this deliverance He's describing is a sure thing. It isn't some "maybe" deal that might happen. No, we can count on God to do this for us every time, all the time. We don't have to worry that He's going to change His mind about it because He never changes.

We also don't have to worry about encountering a problem or a danger that's too big for Him to handle. He isn't just some half-high god. He is the *Most* High. There isn't anything or anyone higher or bigger than Him. He has all the power there is. So,

LIVE FEAR FREE

Jesus can say this without question: *"Surely* He shall deliver you from the snare of the fowler and from the perilous pestilence."

The fowler is the devil. In ancient times, a *fowler* was a person who captured unsuspecting birds, using traps or snares. But the devil is also the one who "fouls" things up. He's the one behind all perilous pestilence. But his foul plans don't stand a chance against you once you've taken refuge in the secret place, because God has taken you under His wing.

Even in the natural, it's a wonderful thing when someone who is good and loving, powerful and successful takes you under his or her wing. It means they're offering you their protection, wisdom, expertise and resources. When God takes you under His wing, He offers you all those things and more.

He not only becomes your place of refuge, He becomes your Provider. His truth and divine wisdom become your "shield and buckler." The word *buckler* is translated *armor* in the Hebrew Bible, and its root means "to go around or encircle." It's used to describe armor because, unlike a shield which provides partial protection, armor totally encircles a person's body. It protects its wearer completely.

This is Covenant talk! When God says He's giving you His armor, He's saying He will provide you with all you could possibly need. He's saying, "You're in My house now; I take care of everything. I have you covered."

FAITH-DEPENDENT PROMISES

If you want to see what it looks like when God has you covered, read in the Bible about Shadrach, Meshach and Abednego. They experienced God's Psalm 91 protection in the midst of a fiery furnace.

As Ashes Under Your Feet

If you've read the story, you'll remember they were sentenced to die in that furnace because they refused a king's order to bow down to a golden idol. Right before they were thrown into the flames, however, they spoke words of faith. They said to the king, "Our God whom we serve is able to deliver us from the burning fiery furnace, and He will deliver us…" (Daniel 3:17).

The king was so infuriated by their confidence in God, he responded to their bold confession of faith by having the furnace heated up seven times more than normal. It was so hot by the time Shadrach, Meshach and Abednego were thrown into it, that the men who tossed them in died from the heat. Shadrach, Meshach and Abednego, however, weren't even singed. God encircled them with His power, kept them safe, and even came and visited with them while they were in the fire!

Looking into the furnace, the king said, "Did we not cast three men bound into the midst of the fire?… I see four men loose, walking in the midst of the fire; and they have no hurt, and the form of the fourth is like the Son of God" (verses 24-25).

God did more than just barely keep Shadrach, Meshach and Abednego alive in that situation. He joined them in it! They didn't have to hop around in the fire trying not to get burned. They strolled around in it with Jesus, just enjoying His presence.

God so completely covered Shadrach, Meshach and Abednego, that when they came walking out of the furnace, they were perfectly fine. They had no burns at all. They didn't even smell like smoke. Even the king wound up praising God in that situation. "There is no other God that can deliver after this sort," he said (verse 29).

In Psalm 91:3-4, Jesus tells us that God has promised the same sort of deliverance to us. In verses 5-10, He says that because

LIVE FEAR FREE

God has provided us with this protection...

> You shall not be afraid of the terror by night, nor of the arrow that flies by day, nor of the pestilence that walks in darkness, nor of the destruction that lays waste at noonday. A thousand may fall at your side, and ten thousand at your right hand; but it shall not come near you. Only with your eyes shall you look, and see the reward of the wicked. Because you have made The LORD, who is my refuge, even the Most High, your dwelling place, no evil shall befall you, nor shall any plague come near your dwelling *(New King James Version).*

When Jesus says there, *You shall not be afraid,* He isn't saying, "Don't worry, darling, you won't be afraid." No, He's giving us a command. Because all God's promises are faith dependent, He's telling us to stand in faith and refuse to fear. He's saying, "You will not be afraid! You will not!"

He's telling us we're not to fear any peril, no matter what it is, or how or when it comes. We're not to fear the terror of the night. That would include threats that arise suddenly, without warning, when they're not expected. We're not to fear the arrow that flies by day, which would include attacks by potentially deadly weapons, which in our day might be anything from flying bullets to bombs to a terrorist attack.

When I think of a sudden, unexpected attack that comes by day, I'm always reminded of the attack on the World Trade Center on September 11, 2001. It was the deadliest terrorist attack ever launched on American soil. Yet God showed up on behalf of His people right in the midst of it, and provided them with supernatural protection.

Gloria and I have a close friend who has a church right there in the financial district, and many of his members worked in those buildings. But because they were well-taught in how to stay in the secret place of the Most High, none of them were killed.

One member of the church was walking right by the Twin Towers just moments before the first plane hit. Suddenly, inside him, he heard the Holy Spirit say, *Run!* Nothing had happened yet. Everything seemed just fine. But he obeyed the prompting of the Spirit anyway and took off running. As a result, when things started exploding and debris started falling, he was far enough away to duck into a subway tunnel where it was safe.

Another member of the church was inside one of the buildings when it collapsed but walked out without a scratch. All around him, people were wounded and covered with ash from the fire, but his clothes were still clean. He didn't even have any soot on him.

We even heard about one woman who started to leave the building just before it collapsed and was told by her supervisor to stay put, that she'd be safe there. But she heard the voice of The LORD inside her say, *Get out of here, and take everyone you can with you.* She did it, and saved not only her own life, but the lives of more than a dozen other people.

Supernatural Immunity and Angels on Assignment

In addition to weapons and attacks of violence, Psalm 91 also tells us we are not to fear pestilences and plagues. It even promises us that no plague will come near our dwelling. Especially in our day, we can be grateful for this because Jesus said one of the signs of the last days will be "pestilences (plagues: malignant and contagious or infectious epidemic diseases which are deadly and devastating)" (Luke 21:11, *Amplified Bible, Classic Edition*).

We've already seen some of these. We're living in a time when

LIVE FEAR FREE

natural sicknesses and diseases aren't the only problem. Now, human beings are actually engineering diseases, and enhancing them for use as bioweapons. But we can stand confidently and fearlessly in faith on Psalm 91 and be delivered from all those diseases. We can live in supernatural health!

One inspiring example of a believer who did this was John G. Lake. An American evangelist, he was serving as a missionary in South Africa in 1910 when a devastating plague swept across the country. In one month, a quarter of the population died. The plague was so contagious, the government couldn't even find anyone willing to bury the dead. They even offered a reward of $1,000 (which was a lot of money at that time) to anyone brave enough to take on the task.

When no volunteers came forward, John G. Lake and his ministry assistants offered to help, free of charge. They went into the plague-stricken homes, brought out the dead and buried them. They came into contact time and again with the germs that caused the disease, yet none of them ever contracted it.

When their immunity to the plague drew the attention of the medical community, John G. Lake offered to let the doctors experiment on him. He let them put living plague germs on his hand and observe through a microscope what took place. The doctors discovered that the germs died the instant they hit Lake's hand.

"It is the law of the spirit of life in Christ Jesus (Romans 8:2)," John G. Lake explained. "I believe that just as long as I keep my soul in contact with the living God, so that His Spirit is flowing into my soul and body, no germ will ever attach itself to me, for the Spirit of God will kill it."

As a born-again, Spirit-filled believer, that same kind of

As Ashes Under Your Feet

immunity is available to you! On the inside, you are wall-to-wall Holy Ghost. He can flow out of your spirit into your body just like He did for John G. Lake. If you'll believe The WORD and cooperate with Him, the Holy Spirit can so surround you with God's protective power that a thousand may fall at your side, and ten thousand at your right hand, and you'll still be left standing.

What's more, because Psalm 91:10 says no evil or plague will come near your dwelling, you can believe God to protect your whole household. You can stand in faith for Him to protect your family, and He'll do it, even if the whole city is falling apart.

> For He shall give His angels charge over you, to keep you in all your ways. In their hands they shall bear you up, lest you dash your foot against a stone (verses 11-12, *New King James Version).*

God's angels, Hebrews 1:14 says, are "ministering spirits, sent forth to minister for them who shall be heirs of salvation." Ministering to and for us is their job. It's what they were created by God to do, and there are more than enough of them to get the job done.

The Bible doesn't tell us exactly how many angels there are, but according to the book of Revelation, there are at least 100 trillion of them. So, there are obviously plenty to go around, and they are extremely powerful. Psalm 103:20 says they "excel in strength" and do The LORD's commandments, "hearkening unto the voice of his WORD."

Your angels are always listening to you! When you say by faith what God says about you, your words become their commands. When you declare the promises in Psalm 91, your angels get busy seeing to it that you don't so much as dash your foot against a stone.

LIVE FEAR FREE

Praise The LORD! Do you see everything you have working for you? You have God's protective armor covering you and encircling you. You have the plague-and-pestilence-slaying power of His Holy Spirit residing in you. You have His WORD and His Spirit giving you wisdom for every situation, and you have angels working for you. No wonder Psalm 91:13 says:

> You shall tread upon the lion and the cobra, the young lion and the serpent you shall trample underfoot (*New King James Version*).

The lion represents frontal attacks by the devil. Those are attacks you know are coming and against which, in the natural, you have no defense. They're like bombings in wartime where, even though you know the bombers are headed your way, you don't have the firepower in the natural to stop them.

When the devil starts dropping bombs on you that you have no natural ability to deal with, you can call on God's ability and trust Him to protect you. You can be like the woman I heard about who lived in London when it was being bombed during World War II. At first, when the bombs started falling and the sirens went off in the night, she would get out of bed and go to the bomb shelter like all her neighbors did. But eventually, she stopped showing up at the shelter.

After a while, one of her neighbors asked her why.

"I don't like it in there," she said. "It's cold and it smells bad."

"But aren't you afraid the bombs will get you?" her neighbor said.

"No. I saw in the Scriptures that God neither slumbers nor sleeps. So, rather than both of us staying awake, I decided I'll just trust Him, stay in bed, and get some sleep." She didn't just decide that on her own, of course. She had gotten a revelation

As Ashes Under Your Feet

from God that He would protect her. She'd heard from Him through His WORD.

If it had been necessary for her to go to the shelter, The LORD would have told her. But it wasn't, and the end of the story proves it. By the time the war was over, bombs had flattened every house on her block…except hers.

That's what it looks like to tread on the lion!

What about trampling the serpent underfoot?

The serpent represents the devil's sneak attacks. Those attacks are like hidden snakes in the grass that try to take you out by catching you unaware. But when you're dwelling in the secret place, the Most High will help you avoid those snakes in the grass. He will come to your defense even before they have a chance to strike.

A dear friend experienced this kind of divine protection when he was serving as a fighter pilot during the war in Vietnam. That war was very different from World War II. In Vietnam, sneak attacks by the enemy were the norm. Viet Cong soldiers generally stayed hidden, then struck unexpectedly with deadly force.

My friend flew F-100s in the Misty Squadron. Heavily involved in intense fighting, this all-volunteer unit of 157 pilots, assigned to fly missions over North Vietnam, often suffered numerous casualties. But my friend was never afraid of dying. He always believed God would take care of him. Although he didn't know much about living by faith back then (he learned about that later, after he went into the ministry) he had read in the Bible about David. "God kept David safe in battle," he said, "and God will keep me."

At one point during his tour of duty, he started repeatedly

LIVE FEAR FREE

having the same dream. It came to him night after night, over and over. He grew so tired of it he'd stay up as late as he could because he didn't want to go to sleep and have the dream again. "It just about drove me out of my mind," he said.

Finally, after about six months the dream stopped coming. Shortly thereafter, the squadron took off on what their commanders said was going to be their highest casualty mission to date. Moments into the mission, my friend realized everything that was happening seemed very familiar.

"Suddenly, I'm knowing where enemy gun emplacements are," he said. "When a couple of our guys went down, I immediately knew where they were. I pinpointed them and got them out. Then I realized, *I'm flying that dream!*"

Against all odds, Misty Squadron didn't lose one man on that mission. Those whose planes went down were rescued. No one was killed!

As soldiers in the last days army of The LORD, we can also experience this kind of Psalm 91 protection. It's not just for fighter pilots and infantry commanders. It's for *every* born-again believer—for mothers, schoolteachers, executives, administrators, students—and anyone else who will believe it.

Jesus was speaking to us all when He made the promises in Psalm 91:3-13. And in the final verses of the psalm, Almighty God, our heavenly Father, speaks and confirms them. He says to Jesus about you, me and every believer to whom these promises are made:

Because he hath set his Love upon me, therefore will I deliver him: I will set him on high, because he hath known my name. He shall call upon me, and I will answer him: I

As Ashes Under Your Feet

will be with him in trouble; I will deliver him, and honour him. With long life will I satisfy him, and show him my salvation (verses 14-16).

Believe it. Speak it. Live fearlessly under the protection of the Almighty in these last days, and until Jesus returns. Be the witness to the gospel this lost world is looking for…and trample the devil as ashes under the soles of your feet!

Prayer for Salvation and Baptism in the Holy Spirit

Heavenly Father, I come to You in the Name of Jesus. Your Word says, "Whosoever shall call on the name of the Lord shall be saved" (Acts 2:21). I am calling on You. I pray and ask Jesus to come into my heart and be Lord over my life according to Romans 10:9-10: "If thou shalt confess with thy mouth the Lord Jesus, and shalt believe in thine heart that God hath raised him from the dead, thou shalt be saved. For with the heart man believeth unto righteousness; and with the mouth confession is made unto salvation." I do that now. I confess that Jesus is Lord, and I believe in my heart that God raised Him from the dead. I repent of sin. I renounce it. I renounce the devil and everything he stands for. Jesus is my Lord.

I am now reborn! I am a Christian—a child of Almighty God! I am saved! You also said in Your Word, "If ye then, being evil, know how to give good gifts unto your children: HOW MUCH MORE shall your heavenly Father give the Holy Spirit to them that ask him?" (Luke 11:13). I'm also asking You to fill me with the Holy Spirit. Holy Spirit, rise up within me as I praise God. I fully expect to speak with other tongues as You give me the utterance (Acts 2:4). In Jesus' Name. Amen!

Begin to praise God for filling you with the Holy Spirit. Speak those words and syllables you receive—not in your own language, but the language given to you by the Holy Spirit. You have to use your own voice. God will not force you to speak. Don't be concerned with how it sounds. It is a heavenly language!

Continue with the blessing God has given you and pray in the spirit every day.

You are a born-again, Spirit-filled believer. You'll never be the same!

Find a good church that boldly preaches God's Word and obeys it. Become part of a church family who will love and care for you as you love and care for them.

We need to be connected to each other. It increases our strength in God. It's God's plan for us.

Make it a habit to watch the *Believer's Voice of Victory* broadcast and VICTORY Channel and become a doer of the Word, who is blessed in his doing (James 1:22-25).

About the Author

Kenneth Copeland is known worldwide as a speaker, teacher, author, television minister and recording artist. Along with his wife, Gloria, he is co-founder of Kenneth Copeland Ministries in Fort Worth, Texas, where for more than 50 years they have passionately taught Christians how to apply the principles of faith found in God's Word in their own lives.

Kenneth is driven by a passion to see people fall in love with Jesus, live by faith in God's Word, and experience victory in every area of life. He ministers around the world—reaching millions with the transforming message of faith and God's love, teaching them that God's Word works, and that Jesus is Lord!

His ministry continues to cover the globe on various platforms. Among those are the *Believer's Voice of Victory* daily and weekly television broadcast; the *Believer's Voice of Victory* monthly magazine; Eagle Mountain International Church; VICTORY Channel, a 24/7 Christian network; and live meetings and conventions. Through Kenneth Copeland Bible College, an accredited Christian Bible school, students are being taught how to live victoriously, and receive understanding of the walk of faith by application of God's Word and His Spirit.

With international offices in Canada, England, Australia, South Africa, Ukraine and Latin America, Kenneth Copeland is fulfilling his God-given vision to boldly preach the uncompromised Word of Faith from the top of the world to the bottom and all the way around the middle.

Learn more about Kenneth Copeland Ministries
by visiting our website at **kcm.org**

BELIEVER'S VOICE OF VICTORY

When the Lord first spoke to Kenneth and Gloria Copeland about starting the *Believer's Voice of Victory* magazine...

He said: *This is your seed. Give it to everyone who ever responds to your ministry, and don't ever allow anyone to pay for a subscription!*

For more than 50 years, it has been the joy of Kenneth Copeland Ministries to bring the good news to believers. Readers enjoy teaching from ministers who write from lives of living contact with God, and testimonies from believers experiencing victory through God's Word in their everyday lives.

Today, the *BVOV* magazine is mailed monthly, bringing encouragement and blessing to believers around the world. Many even use it as a ministry tool, passing it on to others who desire to know Jesus and grow in their faith!

Request your FREE subscription to the
Believer's Voice of Victory **magazine today!**

Go to **freevictory.com** to subscribe online, or call us at **1-800-600-7395** (U.S. only) or **+1-817-852-6000**.

We're Here for You!®

Your growth in God's WORD and victory in Jesus are at the very center of our hearts. In every way God has equipped us, we will help you deal with the issues facing you, so you can be the **victorious overcomer** He has planned for you to be.

The mission of Kenneth Copeland Ministries is about all of us growing and going together. Our prayer is that you will take full advantage of all The LORD has given us to share with you.

Wherever you are in the world, you can watch the *Believer's Voice of Victory* broadcast on television (check your local listings), kcm.org and digital streaming devices like Roku. You can also watch the broadcast as well as programs from dozens of ministers you can trust on our 24/7 faith network—Victory Channel. Visit govictory.com for show listings and all the ways to watch.

Our website, **kcm.org,** gives you access to every resource we've developed for your victory. And, you can find contact information for our international offices in Africa, Australia, Canada, Europe, Ukraine, Latin America and our headquarters in the United States.

Each office is staffed with devoted men and women, ready to serve and pray with you. You can contact the worldwide office nearest you for assistance, and you can call us for prayer at our U.S. number, +1-817-852-6000, every day of the week!

We encourage you to connect with us often and let us be part of your everyday walk of faith!

Jesus Is LORD!

Kenneth and Gloria Copeland